The
New Voices
Nuevas Voces
Guide to Cultural &
Linguistic Diversity
in Early Childhood

The New Voices / Nuevas Voces

Guide to Cultural & Linguistic Diversity in Early Childhood

by

Dina C. Castro, Ph.D., M.P.H.

Betsy Ayankoya, M.Ed.

and

Christina Kasprzak, M.A.

FPG Child Development Institute
The University of North Carolina at Chapel Hill

·PAUL·H·
BROOKES
PUBLISHING Co®

Baltimore • London • Sydney

Paul H. Brookes Publishing Co.
Post Office Box 10624
Baltimore, Maryland 21285-0624
USA

www.brookespublishing.com

Typeset by Matrix Publishing Services, York, Pennsylvania.
Manufactured in the United States of America by
Versa Press, Inc., East Peoria, Illinois.

The New Voices ~ Nuevas Voces Facilitator's Guide to Cultural and Linguistic Diversity in Early Childhood CD-ROM is also available for purchase. To order, contact Brookes Publishing (1-800-638-3775; http://www.brookespublishing.com).

The individuals described in this book are composites or real people whose situations are masked and are based on the author's experiences. Names and identifying details have been changed to protect confidentiality.

Photographs on the cover and the Modules 1 and 5 opening pages by John Cotter. As applicable, photographs are used by the permission of individuals pictured or their parents/guardians.

Permission to use the list of questions and ideas on pages 125–126 from the following is gratefully acknowledged: Santos, R.M., & Reese, D. (1999). *Selecting culturally and linguistically appropriate materials: Suggestions for service providers*. Champaign, IL: ERIC Clearinghouse on Elementary and Early Childhood Education. (ERIC Document Reproduction Service No. ED431546)

Library of Congress Cataloging-in-Publication Data

Castro, Dina Carmela.
    The new voices ~ nuevas voces guide to cultural and linguistic diversity in early childhood / by Dina C. Castro, Betsy Ayankoya, and Christina Kasprzak.
        p.   cm.
    Includes bibliographical references and index.
    ISBN-13: 978-1-59857-046-5 (pbk.)
    ISBN-10: 1-59857-046-3 (pbk.)
    1. Child development—Cross-cultural studies.   2. Early childhood education—
Cross-cultural studies.   3. Multicultural education.   4. Hispanic American children.
5. Children of minorities.   I. Ayankoya, Betsy.   II. Kasprzak, Christina.   III. Title.

HQ767.9.C377 2010
305.231089'68073—dc22   2010016382

British Library Cataloguing in Publication data are available from the British Library.

2014   2013   2012   2011   2010

10   9   8   7   6   5   4   3   2   1

Contents

About the Authors

Dina C. Castro, Ph.D., M.P.H., Senior Scientist, FPG Child Development Institute, The University of North Carolina at Chapel Hill, Campus Box 8180, Chapel Hill, NC 27599-8180

Dr. Castro has 25 years of experience conducting early childhood research, intervention, and program evaluation in the United States and Latin America. She serves as Director of the Center for Early Care and Education Research: Dual Language Learners, funded by the Administration for Children and Families, U.S. Department of Health and Human Services.

Dr. Castro's research focuses on the early care and education of young children who are dual language learners and on children from diverse cultural and ethnic backgrounds, with an emphasis on those living in poverty. She currently serves as Principal Investigator on the study *Nuestros Niños Program: Promoting School Readiness for English Language Learners*, funded by the National Institute for Child Health and Human Development (NICHD). She also directs a study of child care utilization patterns for Latino families funded by the Administration for Children and Families, U.S. Department of Health and Human Services.

Dr. Castro's previous work includes a national study of early childhood programs' policies and practices to address the needs of Latino children and their families, an intervention study to promote early language and literacy among Latino Spanish-speaking children, the development and evaluation of a professional development program on cultural and linguistic diversity for early childhood professionals (New Voices ~ Nuevas Voces), and the evaluation of an Early Head Start initiative to support infants and toddlers who are dual language learners. She also has conducted studies of language and literacy development in young children, factors affecting the well-being of Latino immigrant families, and family involvement in Head Start. Dr. Castro has published numerous articles, book chapters, and reports and presents nationally and internationally as an expert on the early care and education of children who are culturally and linguistically diverse. She is originally from Peru and has lived in the United States since 1991.

Betsy Ayankoya, M.Ed., Educational Planning and Development Consultant, National Early Childhood Technical Assistance Center, FPG Child Development Institute, The University of North Carolina at Chapel Hill, Campus Box 8040, Chapel Hill, NC 27599-8040

Ms. Ayankoya is a native North Carolinian, raised by her maternal grandparents (Rosa F. and John Johnson), who were share croppers, until her early elementary years. Her interest in culture began on that farm with aunts, uncles, and cousins who came for months at a time during harvest seasons. In Washington, D.C., she met her husband, Tai, and they lived for 4½ years in his home community in Ibadan, in Nigeria. Even though it was a different country, the culture of extended family felt very familiar. These experiences, as well as those of their own children, have led to her belief that early life experiences should foster positive self-regard in one's own culture and positive attitudes toward the culture of others.

Since 1992, Ms. Ayankoya has provided consultation to early childhood projects and state administrators in program development, planning, and improvement related to young children with disabilities and their families. She played a key role in two national early intervention personnel preparation projects and served as Co-principal Investigator for New Voices ~ Nuevas Voces. Her work history includes university teaching, conference planning and management, professional development, and training.

Ms. Ayankoya has served on numerous national advisory boards, served on the executive board as past Governor for the Division for Early Childhood (DEC), and served on the Representative Assembly of the Council for Exceptional Children. She currently serves on the DEC multicultural activities, nominations, and awards committees. Her expertise lies in the areas of cultural/linguistic diversity, professional development, family-centered services, and general supervision.

Christina Kasprzak, M.A., Educational Consultant, FPG Child Development Institute, The University of North Carolina at Chapel Hill, Campus Box 8040, Chapel Hill, NC 27599-8040

Christina Kasprzak has more than 12 years of experience in supporting early intervention and early childhood special education programs across the United States in implementing the Individuals with Disabilities Education Act (IDEA). Her technical assistance and training experience has focused on three areas: providing quality services for young children from diverse cultural and linguistic backgrounds, designing and conducting program evaluation, and measuring child and family outcomes for early intervention and early childhood special education programs. Ms. Kasprzak serves as Associate Director of Evaluation for the National Early Childhood Technical Assistance Center. She also is a technical assistance specialist for the Early Childhood Outcomes Center. Ms. Kasprzak was born and raised in Fairfax, Virginia. As a young college student at George Mason University, she began her lifelong passion for reducing poverty and discrimination.

Introduction

Early childhood professionals are finding increasing cultural and linguistic diversity among the children and families they serve. Although the diversity of the children and families has increased, the diversity among professionals has not kept pace with those demographic changes. Therefore, most of the time, early childhood professionals are working with children and families from backgrounds different from their own. In addition, the professional preparation available in higher education programs and the in-service professional development available in the field have not adequately prepared early childhood professionals to work with cultural and linguistically diverse children and families.

The New Voices ~ Nuevas Voces Guide to Cultural and Linguistic Diversity in Early Childhood was developed to respond to the needs of early childhood professionals (teachers, child care providers, home visitors, and early interventionists) and other professionals (physical therapists, psychologists, and speech-language pathologists) working with a population of young children and families that is becoming increasingly diverse. Furthermore, there are new voices in our communities—the voices of culturally and linguistically diverse families—and those voices need to be heard and integrated into our early childhood programs and schools. We need to seek out and listen to these new voices in order to create effective programs that welcome and meet the developmental and learning needs of all children.

The lack of cultural responsiveness in early childhood programs is a challenge in the field of early childhood education and intervention that affects services provided to all children, in particular diverse children and families. The fast growth of the Latino population poses an additional challenge—that is, working with a group that is culturally and linguistically diverse within itself. The Latino population is currently the largest minority group in the United States; however, many professionals have little knowledge about the diversity within the Latino population and may have misconceptions about Latinos' belief systems and practices related to child rearing and education that create barriers for building relationships with these families.

This book includes concepts, strategies, and resources intended to improve professionals' practices when working with culturally and linguistically diverse children and families in general, with a particular emphasis on working with Latino children and their families. Each module is organized to present the general principles and strategies to address cultural and linguistic diversity and then provides additional information specific to working with Latino children and families.

Audience

This book has been developed to help practitioners regardless of their years of experience in the field of early childhood care and education. Participants in the New Voices ~ Nuevas Voces training institutes have ranged from recent graduates to professionals with more than 20 years of experience. What they had in common was their need and desire to gain knowledge and skills to work more effectively with children and families from diverse cultural and linguistic backgrounds, many of them working for the first time with Latino children and families. The book can be used in introductory to intermediate-level professional preparation courses or in-service professional development activities. The content and sequence of the modules were selected to cover the essential information for practitioners to begin their journey into becoming culturally responsive early childhood professionals.

Early childhood professionals and program administrators can work through the guide individually, using it as a self-improvement tool. Program administrators or supervisors can also use the Cultural and Linguistic Diversity in Early Childhood Self-Assessment Scale and the Antibias Observation Checklist at the end of the book (Appendix A and Appendix C, respectively) to monitor staff improvement.

Organization of This Book

The New Voices ~ Nuevas Voces Guide to Cultural and Linguistic Diversity in Early Childhood is divided into five modules designed to address knowledge, attitudes, and skills in five topical areas. Module 1 provides the essential foundations upon which other learning will occur, and the information presented in Module 5 is intended to help integrate the concepts and strategies presented in Modules 1–4. Furthermore, the book has a companion assessment scale (Appendix A) that can be self-administered or can be administered by a trainer, supervisor, professor, or observer to gauge current knowledge, attitudes, and skills and thereby identify strengths or areas for improvement.

We suggest the following steps for using this book:

1. *Assess current beliefs, knowledge, and skills.* Prior to reading and engaging in the activities suggested in the New Voices ~ Nuevas Voces guide, an individual may want to complete the self-assessment scale (Appendix A). The results of this preassessment will be used after completion of the modules for comparison with postassessment results. A facilitator or professor may want to use the scale to assess participants or students and use the results to focus the professional development or course on specific areas of need. In addition, the facilitator or professor may want to use the Antibias Observation Checklist (Appendix C) to gather more detailed information about the environment and practices of teachers and service providers.

2. *Use the book.* Individuals should begin with Module 1. With each module, the following approach is recommended:

   a. Read the text, engage in the suggested activities, and reflect on the embedded personal stories.

   b. Locate and read or view some of the additional resources.

   c. Reflect on new approaches to working with children and families. Consider using the Action Plan form (Appendix D at the end of the book) to record goals, steps to take, time lines, and needed resources.

   d. Try implementing some of the suggested practices, being mindful of current practices. Share and discuss successes and barriers with the facilitator, trainer, or supervisor and/or with colleagues.

3. *Reassess beliefs, knowledge, and skills.* After using the book for a period of time, reassess beliefs, knowledge, and skills using the self-assessment scale (Appendix A) and possibly the observation checklist (Appendix C).

   a. Use a clean version of the self-assessment when completing the scale again.

   b. Compare current answers with previous answers. Identify items where answers have changed.

   c. Compare the new responses to the response key provided in Appendix B. Identify items where responses differ from those provided in the key.

   d. This comparison will yield areas of improvement as well as areas for further information and exploration. Individuals who want to expand their knowledge should review the Recommended Resources sections at the end of each module.

New Voices ~ Nuevas Voces Guiding Principles

1. Everyone is enriched by experiencing diverse cultures. All children enrich the early childhood experience through the diversity of their many origins, beliefs, values, languages, and abilities.

2. Development and learning are embedded in the sociocultural context in which they occur. Learning activities should be meaningful and relevant to each child's experiences.

3. Beliefs and attitudes about culture, language, race, ethnicity, disability, and socioeconomic status have an impact on the way professionals work with and support young children and their families.

4. Understanding families' cultural perspectives is an integral part of family-centered early intervention services and is essential for early education programs to build partnerships with families.

5. Learning to communicate effectively across cultures is a foundation for strengthening early childhood practices and improving results for children and families.

6. Mutual respect for and partnerships between families and early childhood professionals are critical to creating positive outcomes for children.

7. Children's family culture should be encouraged in order to foster development of a positive cultural identity and a healthy social and emotional development.

8. Early childhood experiences should foster positive self-regard in one's own culture and positive attitudes toward the culture of others.

9. Bilingualism is an asset and should be encouraged and supported.

10. Children and families have the right to use and develop their home language. A child's home language serves as the foundation for acquiring new knowledge and for learning a second language.

11. Professional development is most effective when it incorporates individuals' experiences and includes activities that are applicable to real-life situations.

12. Everyone has the capacity to develop skills to work effectively with children and families who have diverse cultures, languages, and abilities.

Acknowledgments

We would like to express our appreciation and gratitude to the New Voices ~ Nuevas Voces project staff who contributed enormously to the formation of the professional development program that gave origin to this book: Romy Allen, Jane Coburn, Mónica Rojas, and Fabiula Unger. We also want to thank Yinka Ayankoya, Anna Levinsohn, and Katushka Olave for their support during the field testing phase.

We are thankful to the Cultural Diversity Committee of the North Carolina Interagency Coordinating Council for serving as the Advisory Board for the New Voices ~ Nuevas Voces project, providing guidance and feedback. Special thanks go to Sherry Franklin and Karen Hass, members of this committee, for their help in reviewing our assessment instrument.

We are grateful to Kathy Baars, former North Carolina 619 Preschool Coordinator, and Dr. Deborah Carroll, North Carolina Early Intervention Branch Head, for supporting the field testing of the professional development program in an effort to provide training to early childhood professionals throughout the state of North Carolina. We thank Anne Marie DeKort-Young, Sherry Franklin, Gasper González, Gay Litton, Meryl Murphy, and Evelyn Seidenberg, who graciously organized and supported New Voices ~ Nuevas Voces training institutes across the state.

We are thankful to our colleagues Dr. Kevin Cole from the Washington Research Institute, Pilar Fort from the Early Head Start National Resource Center at ZERO TO THREE, and Sharon Yandian, who was with the Academy for Educational Development, for their valuable feedback on previous drafts of the book.

Thanks to all of the early childhood professionals from across the country who have participated in New Voices ~ Nuevas Voces training institutes. They have offered us some of the most valuable feedback—that coming from the experience of providing services to young children and families.

We are grateful to all of these individuals who have contributed their time, resources, and expertise to enrich the content of this book that should lead to more culturally and linguistically appropriate services for young children and their families.

A mi familia:
To my mother, Dina, my best teacher and inspiration, for her
humildes consejos that taught me about hard work and social responsibility
To my husband, Jorge, for sharing my dreams and generously
offering his knowledge and wisdom to foster my professional growth
And to my son, Jorge Ernesto, for allowing me to see the world
through his eyes and being the reason for my happiness and pride
—DC

To Elijah, "the best grandson in the whole wide world," from Nan
—BA

To my husband, Jonathan, whose humor,
love, and fabulous cooking I can always count on
And to my former professor, Vickie Rader, who first opened my eyes
to issues of diversity and inspired me to work for justice and equality
—CK

Foundations of Cultural Diversity

NEW VOICES
N V
NUEVAS VOCES

Purpose

To understand the necessary knowledge, attitudes, and skills required for working with young children and families from culturally and linguistically diverse backgrounds, with an emphasis on Latino children and families

Objectives

- Reflect on race, language, and personal culture

- Understand the origin and nature of attitudes toward differences, including disabilities

- Understand the impact of positive and negative attitudes toward differences on children and their families and those who provide services to them

- Acquire knowledge about the Latino population in the United States, including its diversity in terms of national origin, race, ethnicity, and language

Learning to understand and embrace the diversity that is a part of daily life is a continuous process. Acquiring the knowledge and skills necessary to provide education or services that are culturally appropriate takes a lifetime. In fact, we never reach the stage where we have all the answers; however, it is critical that we get to the stage where we know the questions. Those questions should lead us to learn first about ourselves and then to understand others. The process of becoming effective teachers or service providers working with diverse children and families starts with learning about our perceptions of differences, our beliefs and values, and their origin (Banks, 2008).

Usually when we think about diversity, we think not of ourselves but of others and ask questions such as

- How is that person different from me?

- What kind of holidays does he or she celebrate?

- What language does he or she speak?

- What kind of food does he or she eat?

The information included in this module provides an understanding of the principles of diversity from a different perspective, posing a different set of questions—questions that focus on the self. For example,

- What is my cultural heritage?

- What are the circumstances in my life that have shaped my beliefs and values?

- What is important to me?

- How did I come to believe what I do?

- What images do I have about others, and how did my upbringing shape those images?

- How do the attitudes and beliefs that I possess affect the way in which I interact with and provide intervention services to the children and families that I serve?

Learning to provide culturally and linguistically appropriate services and learning about diversity begins with learning about us.

This module follows a sequence of steps to help individuals reflect on personal culture, race, and language; to understand the origin and nature of positive and negative attitudes toward differences; and to see the impact on children and their families and those who provide services to them. Many approaches to diversity training rely on guilt as a motivator to change. According to the theory promoted by the National Coalition Building Institute, "People change more readily when they are lifted up and appreciated, not when they are made to feel guilty" (Brown & Mazza, 1997).

This module also provides information about the Latino population and its characteristics. This material is meant to help increase understanding of the diversity that exists within the Latino population in the United States in terms of national origin, race, ethnicity, and language.

New Voices ~ Nuevas Voces offers professionals an opportunity for in-depth exploration and shares ideas and strategies for developing positive relationships. Professionals will gain needed information to work appropriately with children and families who are from culturally and linguistically diverse backgrounds.

Learning About Similarities and Differences

Understanding cultural diversity requires a thorough look at what you have come to believe about the world and what you have come to value. Where did these beliefs and values come from? Most of our perceptions of the world are shaped by early childhood experiences and factors that are unconscious for the most part. Having an encounter with an individual whose perception of the world differs from yours provides greater awareness of your own perception of the world. See the box that follows for factors that may shape your view of the world.

Engaging in self-reflection can help in developing the ability to connect with others who have no obvious similarities. Reflecting on important identities (e.g., age, gender, race, religion, sexual orientation, disability, ethnicity, nationality, family relationship—sister, parent, mother, father—and so forth) that have shaped your perception of yourself can become a means of understanding your expectations and perception of other people. Every perception is made through your own cultural lens. For example, have you thought that you do not have "culture" because you are Caucasian, middle class, and Protestant? In contrast, have you ever visited another country, hoping to experience local food and ending up surprised because you found hamburgers and Pepsi or Coca-Cola? Why are people from Canada not called Americans? Is *Colorado* an English word? It is actually from the Spanish for *red*, which was applied because of the Colorado River's red appearance. As these questions show, a self-reflection exercise can reveal that many of our presumed truths are actually perceptions.

As a professional who is exploring your own identity, you should take a look at the groups that you belong to. Are there groups that you take for granted or never

▨ Personal Factors that Affect Our Perspectives ▨

—*Place of birth*

—*Birth order*

—*Residence during childhood or adolescence*

—*Gender*

—*Number of children in the family*

—*Religion and its relative importance in the family of origin*

—*Socioeconomic status of the family*

—*Disability or medical condition*

—*Racial, cultural, and ethnic group memberships (see definitions below)*

—*Language(s) (including speaking a language other than English and using sign language)*

Source: Brown and Mazza (1997).

really think about (e.g., being Caucasian, male, or an only child)? Next examine your membership in groups that have had a greater impact on the way you experience your life (e.g., people of color, socioeconomic status, disability). Have you been taught, perhaps by a prejudiced society, that you belong to a particular group? How important is your career or profession to your identity?

Last, explore your identity further by looking closely at less obvious identities that have shaped your perception of the world. Many identities remain hidden because of the lack of acceptance or discrimination by the cultural community in which we reside. Some examples of hidden identities include people with mental or

▨ Definitions of Race, Culture, and Ethnicity ▨

Race *generally refers to social meanings attached to biological or physical characteristics such as skin color, facial features, and hair texture. Racial distinctions are problematic because they are socially constructed and social and biological differences within racial groups are greater than differences between racial groups.*

Culture *refers to meanings and practices that are learned and socially shared. Cultural meanings are produced and enacted by interacting groups of people. Cultural meanings influence "familial roles, communication patterns, affective styles, and values regarding personal control, individualism, collectivism, spirituality and religiosity" (Betancourt & López, 1993, p. 630).*

Ethnicity *refers to groups that share a common history or geography and an identity of themselves as a group.*

Sources: Betancourt and López (1993); D. Skinner (personal communication, January 18, 2010).

■ Our Identities ■

Spend 5–10 minutes thinking about the many groups you belong to, such as race, gender, nationality, religion, sexual orientation, disability, ethnicity, class, and family relationships. Fill in the pieces of the pie with your many identities—for example, woman, mother, African American, middle class, immigrant, teacher, and so forth. Which identities are most important in shaping your life? How has each identity contributed to your view of yourself and people who share that identity, as well as to your view of those who do not share that identity? How has each identity contributed to your view of the world? You may find it interesting to explore this with another person.

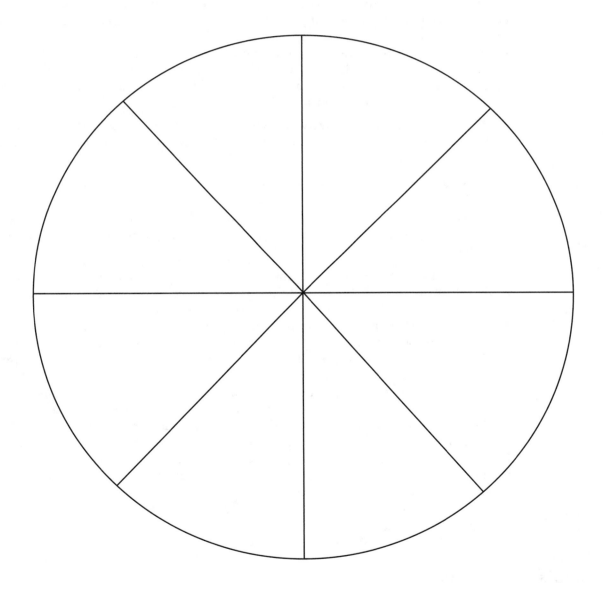

emotional illness, family member of a person with a disability, children who are adopted or in foster care, adult children of alcoholics, individuals with chronic illness, and survivors of abuse or neglect, as well as identities related to sexual orientation. The preceding Our Identities exercise should help you get started on your exploration.

How Stereotypes Develop

Everything that we have heard or been told about another group becomes a part of our internal memory. We learned many of these biases at very young ages from those closest to us—our relatives and peers—as well as from the media. Even when our knowledge and experiences refute these biases, they still exist and can influence our behavior if we are not careful. No one chooses to have these prejudicial ideas, but everyone has them. This does not mean that we are all bigots. It does mean that we need to be aware of how these biases may affect the way we approach others. The comments below are manifestations of prejudice based on stereotypes:

- Some of the parents that we work with don't even have a high school diploma. How can we expect them to be able to make decisions about the type of services that their children need?

- Why does our tax money have to go to take care of people who come here to live off the system?

- The children are struggling and the parents don't show up for meetings. If they really cared about their children, they would be doing everything in their power to help them.

As a consequence of the stereotypes we have learned, we can hold negative biases about our own group that contribute to making us feel less valued or respected. In essence, we internalize the negative messages about ourselves and members of our group. Negative feelings about our own group are referred to as internalized oppression. Internalized oppression often begins in childhood and has a detrimental effect on the individual and entire groups of people. Internalized oppression is also expressed through infighting or lack of harmony within groups and between oppressed groups.

Not all of the stereotypes that people hold are negative. There are also positive stereotypes (e.g., certain groups of people make better students, athletes, lovers, or dancers). Yet, even these positive stereotypes can cause harm to the individual because they lead to idealizing, having unrealistic expectations, or romanticizing. Both negative and positive stereotypes prevent the viewer from seeing and getting to know the real person. The following material is designed to help you learn more about yourself and, in turn, to understand feelings and reactions when interacting with unfamiliar people and environments. You may want to journal about the questions posed in each section.

Impacts on Children

What is the impact of our attitudes on the children and families that we serve? Our attitudes and perceptions are infused into every interaction that we have and into everything that we do. Even if we are not aware of our own preconceived ideas and biases, we reflect them when we relate to the children in our care. As a consequence, these ideas and biases may negatively influence our relationship with particular families and, moreover, children's identity and self-esteem.

Identity Development

Identity is an internalized self-selected concept based on one's experiences and interactions, both inside and outside the family. Given this definition, when do children actually develop a sense of identity?

Children develop awareness of differences in stages (see Table 1.1 for a summary). Young infants can distinguish smells, recognize voices, and feel attachment to familiar smells and voices. Within the first few months of life, they develop an awareness of strangers, can observe differences and similarities, and have a sense of being cared for. By age 2–3 years, children develop an awareness of gender, begin to recognize ethnic differences, and recognize colors—recognizing not only their own color but also talking about how it differs from that of other people. By this age, children may even show signs of "preprejudice" on the basis of gender, race, or ability. Awareness of disabilities tends to come later in children; however, some toddlers begin noticing more obvious disabilities, such as a person using a cane or a wheelchair. By age 3–4, children know how to categorize people—that is, they can tell the differences between boys and girls, skin colors, hair textures, and eye shapes. By age 5, children begin to build a group ethnic identity and an individual identity. They are also able to understand and explore differences and similarities between ethnic groups (Derman-Sparks, 1989).

In their daily interactions with peers and adults, children receive messages about which characteristics are valued and encouraged in a particular context or situation and which are not. For example, a teacher who refuses to pay attention to a child who is speaking a language other than English in the classroom is sending this child the message that his or her home language is not valued. Similarly, if the classroom environment does not incorporate cultural elements other than those related to the mainstream culture, the message for culturally diverse children is that their cultural heritage is not valued. Teachers and caregivers are more aware that these concerns are equally important for all children. Derman-Sparks and Ramsey (2005) pointed out, "Many teachers of young children now have become more aware of how racism affects white children as well as children of color. They understand that a false sense of superiority is isolating and damaging and poorly prepares white children to function in a diverse society" (p. 20).

What can early childhood professionals do to support children in their identity development? Professionals first need to be aware of how children develop identity

Table 1.1. When young children develop awareness of differences

Infants	Distinguish smells and recognize voices
Age 2–3	Awareness of gender, ethnic differences, and colors
Age 3–4	Categorize people by gender, skin colors, hair textures, and eye shapes
By age 5	Build an individual identity and group ethnic identity; understand similarities and differences between ethnic groups

October 9, 2001

This day was the tenth anniversary of my family's departure from Peru. That day ten years ago marked the start of a new life. I realized while going over our family's history in the United States in my mind how much we've accomplished and how hard my parents have had to struggle to reach the level we now have as a family. We have managed to construct a new universe for ourselves in a sometimes hostile place, with new friends and new opportunities, but at the same time new obstacles.

Finally, I have come to see that even though I am extremely close to my family, we now differ in thoughts of home. For my parents, Lima, Peru, will always be home, but for me, Lima is where I come from, and it is where my beloved family and culture are rooted, but it is not my home.

My home is here in Raleigh; my life is centered here. Ten years in a new country have done that to me. My formation is a joint project between a bustling metropolis teeming with life (Lima has 8 million inhabitants) and a small, quaint little town in suburban North Carolina.

—Mario, 14 years old

and second should create a setting rich in possibilities for exploring cultural diversity. There are tremendous opportunities in everyday routines that allow children to explore cultural diversity. Embedding opportunities, whether in a classroom or while working individually with children and families, avoids having what one Native American called "Teepee Day," where all the stereotypes are rolled out. It is also important for professionals to address modern culture rather than celebrations of a historical or "festival" nature. The experience of immigrant children with regard to identity development is particularly challenging. Not only do they have to learn a new language, but they also have to learn a new set of social rules and expectations. Depending on their experiences in their new setting, they will develop a healthy bicultural identity or will end up rejecting their heritage.

The preceding story was written by Mario at age 14. Mario was 4 years old when he arrived in the United States with his parents. His story gives some insight into the development of his identity as a child of immigrant parents. Think about the words that he uses to describe the life that he and his family have experienced. Have the children in your care experienced a life similar to this?

Mario's story speaks about how his thoughts differ from those of his parents as a result of living in the United States for 10 years. This change in attitude, cultural identity, and behavior that occurs following intercultural contact is a process known as acculturation (Berry, 2003). See Table 1.2 for more information about acculturation.

Table 1.2. Four profiles of acculturation

Assimilation	Little interest in cultural maintenance with a preference for interacting with the new or host culture
Separation	Cultural maintenance while avoiding involvement and interaction with new or host culture
Marginalization	Neither maintenance of heritage culture nor interaction with others in new or host culture
Integration	Maintaining cultural identity of heritage culture while interacting with the new or host culture

Source: Berry, Phinney, Sam, and Vedder (2006).

Many factors contribute to the level of acculturation, including amount of time residing in the new culture, age of introduction to the new culture, and among others, the amount of support and encouragement for immigrants to pursue integration. According to Berry, Phinney, Sam, and Vedder (2006), the relationship between how immigrant youth acculturate and how well they adapt to this acculturation process may affect their psychological and social well-being. Using two different statistical approaches, they found that being involved in both the heritage culture and the larger society—that is, integration—resulted in more positive psychological and social outcomes. Concerted effort to maintain heritage language and culture while adopting the new or host language and culture resulted in the best outcomes. In contrast, the amount of discrimination aimed at the immigrant group was strongly related to poor adaptation. The study stressed that integration leads to overall quality of life for "immigrant-receiving societies"—that is, there were positive outcomes for both the immigrant populations and the host cultures.

Creating early childhood environments that support the best outcomes for all children is the focus of *New Voices ~ Nuevas Voces*. All children are best served when we pay attention to cultural diversity and inclusion. Strategies provided later in this manual address the challenges faced by professionals and families and provide approaches to ensure positive outcomes for all children.

Hispanics or Latinos?

Era la primera vez que me clasificaban como latina o hispana y he vivido en Europa y en Europa cuando me preguntaban, yo decía que era colombiana o latinoamericana, pero no usaba ningún término específico, nunca "latina," nunca "hispana," es la primera vez para mí [aquí en los Estados Unidos]. Para mí hispano es más relacionado e incluye a España. Cuando es hispano, incluyen los descendientes españoles. Con el término latino si me refiero hacia Latinoamérica o Sudamérica, podría estar más cerca el término latino, ¿no? . . . pero tampoco es . . . inclusive, [depende] de la manera que es tratado "latino," entonces "latino" o "hispano" es confuso. Lo que me indigna es que me colocan en una caja, me colocan, "Eres hispana," o sea que no tengo lugar a defenderme, como por ejemplo: Mi familia por parte de madre viene de Italia, pero no tengo lugar a defenderme, soy hispana. No reconocen

It was the first time I was classified as Latina or Hispanic, and I have lived in Europe. In Europe when someone asked me, I said that I was Columbian or Latin American, but I did not use any specific term, never "Latina" or "Hispanic." It is the first time for me [here in the United States]. For me "Hispanic" is more related to and includes Spain. When someone is Hispanic, that includes those who descend from the Spaniards. With the term "Latino," if I am referring to Latin America or South America, the term "Latino" could be closer, right? But no, it isn't either. It depends on the way in which "Latino" is used. Then "Latino" or "Hispanic" is confusing. What angers me the most is to be placed in a box, they put me "You are Hispanic," so that I don't have the right to defend myself. For example, my family from my mother's side comes from Italy, but I cannot defend myself, they insist "I am Hispanic." It is not recognized, and

y no lo ven además, como està
confluido en mi piel canela, no se ve.
    Me sigo considerando Columbiana,
pero como se dice, "si vas a Roma, hay
que hacer lo que los romanos hacen."
Sé que en términos de comunicación
para la sociedad americana, tengo que
denominarme hispana o latina.

it is not seen because is mingled in my
cinnamon-colored skin.
    I still consider myself Colombian,
but as it is said "If you go to Rome,
do what the Romans do." I know that
in terms of communication in the
American society, I have to call myself
Hispanic or Latina.

—Claudia, Colombia

Hasta ahora no consigo clasificarme o ponerme en una caja.

[Even now, I still have difficulty classifying myself or putting myself in a box.]

If you are confused about the terms used to identify the fast growing, largest minority population in the United States, you are not alone. The terms that have been used most recently are *Hispanic* and *Latino*. Although the terms are used interchangeably, they do not have exactly the same meaning.

For the first time, in the 1970 U.S. Census, a separate question on Hispanic origin or descent was asked, but only of a 5% sample of the population. In areas with a substantial number of Spanish-speaking households, a Spanish language version of the instruction sheet was also enclosed. In the 1980 Census, a question on Spanish or Hispanic origin or descent was added to 100% of questions for the first time (U.S. Census Bureau, 2010).

Latino is a more inclusive term that does not de-emphasize the crucial role of indigenous Indian cultures, African slaves, and Asian and other immigrant populations in Latin American history.

In the 2000 Census, the term *Latino* was added to the question about Hispanic origin; therefore, both terms are now used interchangeably to refer to

> Those people who classified themselves in one of the specific Spanish, Hispanic, or Latino categories listed on the Census 2000 questionnaire—"Mexican, Mexican American, Chicano," "Puerto Rican," or "Cuban"—as well as those who indicate that they are "other Spanish/Hispanic/Latino." Persons who indicated that they are "other Spanish/Hispanic/Latino" include those whose origins are from Spain, the Spanish-speaking countries of Central or South America, the Dominican Republic or people identifying themselves generally as Spanish, Spanish-American, Hispanic, Hispano, Latino, and so on. (U.S. Census Bureau, 2007)

Origin can be viewed as the heritage, nationality group, lineage, or country of birth of the person or the person's parents or ancestors before their arrival in the United States. People who identify their origin as Spanish, Hispanic, or Latino may be of any race. The Hispanic or Latino population consists of people coming from, or with heritage from, more than 20 countries in North, Central, and South America; the Caribbean; and Spain.

Most Latinos would not be familiar with these terms until arriving in the United States, and they would probably feel more comfortable being identified by their national origin, as Juana explained:

En México no usamos [ni hispano, ni latino]. Pues, en México nos decimos mexicanos o depende de la ciudad que vengas dentro de México. Cuando platicábamos, nunca nos metíamos con las palabras, "hispano" o "latino," pues allá te preguntan de dónde eres y uno responde del país que viene.

We don't use it ["Hispanic" or "Latino"] in Mexico. Well, in Mexico we call ourselves Mexicans, or it depends on the city within Mexico that you come from. When we talked, we never used these words, "Hispanic" or "Latino," since over there they ask you where you are from and one responds with the country one comes from.

For Latino immigrants like Claudia, it takes time getting accustomed to use these words in referring to themselves:

Es difícil porque estás entrando a un país donde no es tu idioma, no naciste aquí, y tienes que aprender todo el sistema, encima tienes que aprender que no eres lo que creías que eras.

It's difficult because you are entering a country where it's not your language, you weren't born here, and you have to learn the whole system, and on top of that you have to learn that you aren't what you thought you were....

For many people, it does not matter which word is used because neither word has meaning for them. Elizabeth expresses this idea:

Yo los había escuchado antes en Puerto Rico, pues, gente en Puerto Rico los usa mucho porque hay mucha influencia de los Estados Unidos. Para mí, los dos describen el latino igual, no sé la diferencia. Para mí, me da igual. Ninguno de los dos está ni mal ni bien. Yo no sé la diferencia. Ni es mal o bueno, yo misma los uso indiscriminadamente.

I had heard them before because in Puerto Rico, well, people in Puerto Rico, use them a lot because there is a lot of influence from the United States. To me, they both describe the Latino the same; I don't know the difference. For me, they are the same. Neither of them is either bad or good. I myself use them indiscriminately.

However, when asked if she considered herself Latina or Hispanic or preferred another term, she responded:

Puertorriqueña. Pero, cuando te piden el origen pongo hispana, pues, porque hablo español.

Puerto Rican. But when they ask for your origin I put Hispanic, well, because [I] speak Spanish.

Most individuals from Latin American countries use their country of origin to identify themselves. For example, one might say that he or she is Mexican, Guatemalan, or Salvadorian. For many Latino immigrants, the first time they encounter the terms *Hispanic* or *Latino* will be when they enter the United States and need to indicate their race or ethnicity on a form. Leticia's story shows how she learned about these terms:

At the airport, when I first arrived in the United States with my husband, the immigration officer gave me papers to complete. When I got to the box asking for race, I checked "White." My husband, who is an American, said, "No, you are not white," and I answered, "What do you mean, I'm not white? I've always been white." He replied, "Here in the U.S., you are 'Hispanic.'" That is when I learned that even though I have light skin, in the United States, I am not white, I am Hispanic. That was very confusing.

Depending on the geographic area, national origin, or generation, Hispanics/Latinos may prefer one term over the other. The division in usage seems as much related to geography as it is to politics, with *Latino* widely preferred in California and *Hispanic* more often used in Florida and Texas. Even in these areas, however, usage is often mixed, and it is not uncommon to find both terms used by the same writer or speaker.

In addition to these two terms, there are others that are used, and actually preferred, by individuals of Mexican origin who have lived in California and the Southwest for centuries. About 150 years ago, approximately 50% of what was then Mexico was appropriated by the United States as a consequence of the U.S. victory in the U.S.–Mexican war. Mexican citizens living in that territory became citizens of the United States overnight. The Treaty of Guadalupe Hidalgo, declaring peace between the two countries, recognized the rights of those people to their private properties (as deeded by Mexican or Spanish colonial authorities), to their own religion (Catholicism), and to speak and receive education in their own language (for the majority, Spanish) (Griswold Del Castillo, 1990). The descendants of this population call themselves Mexican Americans or Chicanos. The term *Mexican American* is more commonly used to recognize U.S. citizens who are descendants of Mexicans. The term *Chicano* was adopted by Mexican American activists who took part in the Brown Power movement of the 1960s and 1970s in the Southwest and has now come into widespread usage (Hurtado & Gurin, 2004). This term is preferred by political activists and by those who seek to create a unique identity for their culture, which, while being strongly tied to their Mexican roots, has new elements that differentiate them from recent Mexican immigrants.

So, Who Are the Latinos?

Latinos are an ethnic group (referring to cultural origins) rather than a racial group (referring to biological or physical characteristics). In fact most Latinos have diverse racial backgrounds and are considered mestizos. Mestizaje is the process of racial mixtures generated by interracial marriages. This started during the colonial days and continues. Because of this diverse heritage, most Latinos cannot claim to belong to one particular race, nor may they desire to do so.

Since the late 1990s, the Latino population has experienced a large growth. Currently, Latinos are the largest minority group in the United States, estimated at 14.4% of the population (U.S. Census Bureau, 2006). The percentage of Latinos is even larger among young children, with 23% of all babies born in the country in 2004 to Latino mothers. Among children younger than 5 years of age, Latinos make up 21.4% of the total population. Furthermore, among children in poverty, Latinos comprise 33.9% (U.S. Census Bureau, 2004a). The greatest increases in the Latino population occurred in the southeastern states, with a reported increase of up to 400% in North Carolina and Georgia (U.S. Census Bureau, Population Division, Ethnic and Hispanic Statistics Branch, 2003). These estimates do not include migrant farm workers. Most Latinos in the United States are of Mexican descent (59%), with Puerto Ricans being 9.7% and those of Cuban origin 3.5%. The last Census shows an increase in the number of Latinos who are from Central and South American countries; they constitute 9.1% of the Latino population. Within this group, individuals with origins in El Salvador, Guatemala, Colombia, Ecuador, and Peru have the largest numbers. Another group that has grown significantly in the last decade are people from the Dominican Republic; they constitute 2.3% of the Latinos. Other estimations from the U.S. Census Bureau show that of all foreign-born individuals in the United States, 51% are from Latin America. However, most Latinos (more than 70%) are U.S.-born or foreign-born naturalized citizens; although recent immigrants make up a smaller percentage and among them, most are legal residents.

Spanish is the language spoken at home among most Latinos; however, there are many other languages spoken at home, such as Portuguese (e.g., spoken by families from Brazil) and hundreds of indigenous languages from Mexico, Central America, and South America (e.g., Otomí, Chatino, Nahuatl, Quechua, Guaraní). The use of Spanish varies among Latino families, depending on the length of time living in the United States and the generations involved. In 2000, more than 75% of Latinos spoke a language other than English at home, and 99% of them spoke Spanish (U.S. Census Bureau, 2004b).

The majority of Latinos are proficient in English. A survey conducted with a representative national sample of Latinos reported that 60% of Latino adults spoke English "pretty well" or "very well." Among them, 96% of U.S.-born Latinos reported speaking English "pretty well" or "very well," compared with 38% of foreign-born Latinos (Pew Hispanic Center/Henry J. Kaiser Family Foundation, 2002).

Other characteristics of the Latino population include having the highest fertility rates of any racial or ethnic group within the United States, which indicates that the growth of the Latino population cannot be explained only by immigration (Martin et al., 2005). By the beginning of the 21st century, Latino children became the largest minority child population in the country (Ramírez & de la Cruz, 2003).

With regard to access to early childhood education, Latino children are less likely to be enrolled in an early childhood program than other groups (U.S. Department of Education, National Center for Education Statistics [NCES], 2000). The rates are nearly the same in urban and suburban areas. In addition, research has shown that Latino families are not gaining access to and utilizing early intervention and other health and social services as frequently as families from other racial and/or ethnic groups. Also, Latino families report greater needs for information about how to get services, compared with parents in other ethnic groups, and a greater level of need overall (see, e.g., Arcia, Keyes, Gallagher, & Herrick,1993; Bailey, Skinner, Rodriguez, Gut, & Correa, 1999; Sontag & Schacht, 1994).

The lower participation rate of Latino children in early childhood programs does not account entirely for the disparity that exists between Latino children and other groups with respect to school readiness. Even among those who have attended preschool, Latino children lag behind their peers when they enter kindergarten, and the gap in academic achievement appears to widen as children grow older. Among 3- to 5-year-olds not yet enrolled in kindergarten, Caucasian and African American children are more likely than Latinos to recognize most letters of the alphabet, participate in storybook activities, count up to at least 20, and write or draw rather than scribble (U.S. Department of Education, 2000). Latino kindergartners have been reported to obtain the lowest performance in reading proficiency compared to African American, Asian, and Caucasian children (West, Denton, & Reaney, 2000).

Because the Latino population is young (median age = 26 years), agencies providing services to young children and their families—such as early intervention services, maternal and child health clinics, and Head Start and other preschool programs—have experienced a significant rise in the number of Latino children and families they serve. Many early childhood professionals have had only limited experience interacting and working with Latino children and families. Furthermore, they may not have received any preparation during their professional training on working with diverse groups of children in general and Latino children in particular.

Getting back to the role of your perceptions on your actions, knowing about your perceptions of the Latino culture would be the first step in the process to learn how to work effectively with this population. The Perceptions of the Hispanic/ Latino Culture activity is intended to help you get started.

After you complete the Perceptions of the Hispanic/Latino Culture activity, conclude this module by conducting a self-assessment of your beliefs, knowledge, and actions regarding cultural and linguistic diversity in early childhood. Fill out a copy of the Cultural and Linguistic Diversity in Early Childhood Self-Assessment Scale, found in Appendix A at the end of the book. Then, refer to the response key in Appendix B. The key provides the ideal responses for each portion of the scale. Comparing your answers to the key will give you an idea of areas of strength and areas to focus on for more growth.

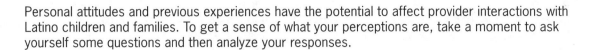

Perceptions of the Hispanic/Latino Culture

Personal attitudes and previous experiences have the potential to affect provider interactions with Latino children and families. To get a sense of what your perceptions are, take a moment to ask yourself some questions and then analyze your responses.

1. When you were growing up, where did you first hear about Hispanic/Latino people? What did you hear or see?

2. Did you have any friends or acquaintances who were Hispanic/Latino? Briefly, what was your experience with them?

3. What similarities and differences are there between Hispanic/Latino families and your family?

4. How do you think stereotypes about Hispanic/Latino families might affect the way service providers work with them and their children?

Conclusion

The intent of Module 1 has been to help individuals reflect on their own culture, race, and language. Material was provided to assist readers in understanding the origin and nature of attitudes toward differences. In turn, readers were encouraged to understand the impact of positive and negative attitudes toward differences on children and their families and those who provide services to them. Module 1 also presented material to help individuals understand the diversity within the Latino population in the United States in terms of national origin, race, ethnicity, and language. Finally, readers were given the opportunity to assess their own knowledge of, attitudes about, and practices with diverse children and families.

Key Ideas to Remember

- Your personal experience and identity contribute to the way you view the world and your place in it.
- Your cultural beliefs affect the way you serve children and families that are from cultures different from your own.
- Teachers and providers should be aware of the cultural and linguistic backgrounds of the children and families they serve in order to provide effective services.
- Early childhood professionals can support children in their identity development by becoming aware of the stages of identity development and using opportunities in everyday routines that allow children to explore cultural diversity.
- It is important to participate in activities for learning about other cultures (e.g., take courses, read books, visit community programs, attend cultural festivals and community events).
- The terms *Hispanic* and *Latino* designate an ethnic group (referring to cultural origins) rather than a racial group (referring to biological or physical characteristics).
- The term *Hispanic* was first used by the U.S. Census Bureau in 1970 to identify people whose heritage can be traced to any Spanish-speaking country; however, most individuals from Latin American countries use their country of origin to identify themselves.
- Mexicans make up the largest percentage of Hispanics/Latinos in the United States.
- U.S.-born people of Mexican descent (particularly in California and the Southwest) often prefer to identify themselves with the terms *Mexican American* or *Chicano.*
- Spanish is the most widely spoken language among Latinos; however, other languages spoken among Latinos include Portuguese (spoken by individuals from Brazil) and indigenous languages.
- More than half of Hispanics/Latinos living in the U.S. are high school graduates.

Reflecting and Getting Ready for Change

See the recommended readings, videotapes, and web sites at the end of this module for resources on your journey to become a more culturally responsive and therefore a more effective teacher or service provider in your work with culturally and linguistically diverse children and families. Before going on to the next module, this is a good time to revisit the questions that were asked at the beginning of Module 1:

1. What is my cultural heritage?

2. What are the things in my life that have shaped my beliefs and values?

3. What is important to me?

4. How did I come to believe that this is important?

5. What images do I have about others, and how did my upbringing shape those images?

6. How do the attitudes and beliefs that I possess affect the way in which I interact and provide intervention services to the children and families that I serve?

In further exploration, think about your work with the families in your program by writing down your answers to the following additional questions:

7. When I think about the families I serve, what comes first to my mind?

8. Are some of these thoughts negative? What are they?

9. What are the positive thoughts that I have about the groups to which these families belong?

10. How do these thoughts affect my attitudes about each family?

11. What are the steps I will take to work on my negative attitudes?

12. Do I need more information or assistance?

13. Who will I ask to help me?

14. What steps will I take to get to know each family better?

References

Arcia, E., Keyes, L., Gallagher, J.J., & Herrick, H. (1993). National portrait of sociodemographic factors associated with underutilization of services: Relevance to early intervention. *Journal of Early Intervention, 17,* 283–297.

Bailey, D., Skinner, D., Rodriguez, P., Gut, D., & Correa, V. (1999). Awareness, use, and satisfaction with services for Latino parents of young children with disabilities. *Exceptional Children, 65,* 367–381.

Banks, J.A. (2008). *An introduction to multicultural education* (4th ed.). Boston: Allyn & Bacon.

Berry, J.W. (2003). Conceptual approaches to acculturation. In K. Chun, P. Balls-Organista, & G. Marin (Eds.), *Acculturation: Advances in theory, measurement and applied research* (pp.17–37). Washington, DC: American Psychological Association Press.

Berry, J.W., Phinney, J.S., Sam, D.L., & Vedder, P. (2006). Immigrant youth: Acculturation, identity, and adaptation. *Applied Psychology: An International Review, 55*(3), 303–332.

Betancourt, H., & López, S.R. (1993). The study of culture, ethnicity, and race in American psychology. *American Psychologist, 48*(6), 629–637.

Brown v. Board of Education, 347 U.S. 483 (1954).

Brown, C., & Mazza, G. (1997). *Healing into action: A leadership guide for creating diverse communities.* Washington, DC: National Coalition Building Institute.

Bucher, R. (2004). *Diversity consciousness: Opening our minds to people, cultures and opportunities* (2nd ed.). Upper Saddle River, NJ: Prentice Hall.

Derman-Sparks, L. (1989). *Anti-bias curriculum: Tools for empowering young children.* Washington, DC: National Association for the Education of Young Children.

Derman-Sparks, L., & Brunson-Phillips, C. (1997). *Teaching/learning anti-racism: A developmental approach.* New York: Teachers College Press.

Derman-Sparks, L., & Ramsey, P. (2005). What if all the children in my class are white? Anti-bias/multicultural education with white children. *Young Children, 60*(6), 20–27.

Griswold Del Castillo, R. (1990). *The Treaty of Guadalupe Hidalgo: A legacy of conflict.* Norman: University of Oklahoma Press.

Hurtado, A., & Gurin, P. (2004). *Chicana/o identity in a changing U.S. society.* Tucson: University of Arizona Press.

Kral, B. (2000). The eyes of Jane Elliott. *Horizon* [Electronic version] Retrieved June 1, 2004, from http://www.horizonmag.com/4/jane-elliott.asp

Martin, J.A., Hamilton, B.E., Sutton, P.E., Ventura, S.J., Menacker, F., & Munson, M.S. (2005). Births: Final data for 2003. *National Vital Statistics Report, 52*(2), 1–114.

McIntosh, P. (1988). *White privilege and male privilege: A personal account of coming to see correspondences through work in women's studies* (Working paper 189).Wellesley, MA: Wellesley College Center for Research on Women.

National Coalition Building Institute. (2003). *Principles into practice: Strengthening leadership for a diverse society.* Washington, DC: Author.

Pew Hispanic Center/Kaiser Family Foundation. (2002). *2002 national survey of Latinos.* Menlo Park, CA, and Washington, DC: Author.

Ramírez, R.R., & de la Cruz, G.P. (2003). The Hispanic population in the United States: March 2002. *Current Population Reports,* P20–545.

Sontag, J.C., & Schacht, R. (1994). An ethnic comparison of parent participation and information needs in early intervention. *Exceptional Children, 60*(5), 422–433.

Tannen, D. (1990). *You just don't understand.* New York: Ballantine Books.

U.S. Census Bureau. (2004a). *Current population survey: Annual social and economic supplement.* Washington, DC: Author.

U.S. Census Bureau. (2004b). *We the people: Hispanics in the United States. Census 2000 special reports.* Washington, DC: U.S. Department of Commerce.

U.S. Census Bureau. (2006, May 10). *Nation's population one-third minority* [press release]. Washington, DC: Author.

U.S. Census Bureau. (2007). *County population estimates by demographic characteristics— age, sex, race, and Hispanic origin; updated annually for states and counties. Persons of Hispanic or Latino origin, percent, 2007.* Retrieved January 11, 2010, from http://quickfacts. census.gov/qfd/meta/long_RHI725208.htm

U.S. Census Bureau. (2010). *1980 overview.* Retrieved March 24, 2010, from http://www. census.gov/history/www/through_the_decades/overview/1980.html

U.S. Census Bureau, Population Division, Ethnic and Hispanic Statistics Branch. (2003). *Hispanic population of the U.S.* Retrieved November 5, 2008, from http://www.census.gov/ population/www/socdemo/hispanic.html

U.S. Department of Education, National Center for Educational Statistics. (2000). *Statistics in brief—March 2000: Home literacy activities and signs of children's emerging literacy, 1993–1999.* Washington, DC: U.S. Government Printing Office.

Van Ausdale, D., & Feagin, J.R. (2001). *The first R: How children learn race and racism.* Lanham, MD: Rowman and Littlefield Publishers.

West, J., Denton, K., & Reaney, L.M. (2000). *The kindergarten year: Findings from the Early Childhood Longitudinal Study, kindergarten class of 1998–99* [Report # 2001023]. Washington, DC: U.S. Department of Education, National Center for Educational Statistics.

Recommended Resources

Books and Videos

Aliotta, J.J., & Stotsky, S. (1996). *The Puerto Ricans.* New York: Chelsea House Publishers.

This is part of Chelsea House Publishers' The Immigrant Experience series. This book examines the history, culture, and religion of the Puerto Ricans; their place in American society; and their achievements up to the present.

Barrera, I., Corso, R.M., &, Macpherson, D. (2003). *Skilled Dialogue: Strategies for responding to cultural diversity in early childhood.* Baltimore: Paul H. Brookes Publishing Co.

This book provides a model for understanding culture and diversity. It also provides strategies for learning and applying the essentials of Skilled Dialogue.

Benson, S., & Kanellos, N. (2002). *The Hispanic-American almanac: A reference work on Hispanics in the United States.* Detroit, MI: Gale Cengage.

This reference tool provides an overview of the history of Hispanics from the Spanish conquests in the New World to the modern emigrations to the United States, including a chronology and copies of major historic documents. It describes the legal and political history of Hispanics. This reference also contains biographical information of Spanish explorers, sports figures, television personalities, artists, advertising executives, and scientists.

Brown, C.R., & Mazza, G.J. (1997). *Healing into action: A leadership guide for creating diverse communities.* Washington, DC: National Coalition Building Institute.

Through theories, examples, and activities, numerous principles are discussed. Topics addressed are building environments to welcome diversity, healing ourselves to change the world, becoming effective allies, and empowering leaders to lead.

Bucher, R. (2004). *Diversity consciousness: Opening our minds to people, cultures and opportunities.* Upper Saddle River, NJ: Prentice Hall.

This is a useful guide for raising diversity consciousness, and it discusses how being open to other cultures is necessary for a quality education and successful career. This book offers a wide variety of real-life student experiences and perspectives throughout the book, along with self-reflective journal questions and interactive exercises. Current discussions on diversity and workplace issues help the reader positively and effectively deal with a variety of diversity issues in the workplace.

California Tomorrow. (2003). *No more lies, no more shame* [Curriculum]. Oakland, CA: Author.

This curriculum is for progressive educators and organizers who work with youth and are interested in exploring cultural stereotypes, colonization, identity politics, and oppression and resistance.

Carlson, L.M. (2005). *Red hot salsa: Bilingual poems on being young and Latino in the United States.* New York: Henry Holt and Company.

This collection of poems celebrates the tones, rhythms, sounds, and experiences of growing up Latino in America, straddling languages, cultures, and identities.

Chang, H., Salazar, D., & Leong, C. (1994). *Drawing strength from diversity: Effective services for youth and families.* Oakland: California Tomorrow.

Drawing Strength from Diversity builds on the foundation being laid by current human services reform efforts, which focus on interagency collaboration, community decision making, creative financing, and improved outcomes, among other strategies.

Deedy, C.A. (2004). *Growing up Cuban in Decatur, Georgia.* Atlanta: Peachtree Publishers.

The author shares funny, warm, and loving stories of her memories of growing up in Decatur, Georgia, after her family emigrated from Havana, Cuba.

Derman-Sparks, L., & Brunson-Philips, C. (1997). *Teaching/learning anti-racism: A developmental approach.* New York: Teachers College Press.

This book explains the interaction between teachers and students as they grapple with learning about racism and become antiracist. It describes the conceptual framework for antiracism and the premises underlying the researchers' pedagogy. It describes the course Racism and Human Development and, through student writings, shows how each class session contributes to the progression of students' growth from proracism to active antiracism.

Gomez, L. (2008). *Manifest destinies: The making of the Mexican American race*. New York: New York University Press.

This book traces the origins of Mexican Americans as a race and explores the historic shift in the meaning of race and how people would be treated by the law according to race.

Grieshaber, S., & Cannella, G.S. (2001). *Embracing identities in early childhood education: Diversity and possibilities*. New York: Teacher's College Press.

This book draws on the work of early childhood teachers and teacher educators and provides examples of creative ways in which practitioners and theorists are rethinking their work. The thinking, theorizing, and practical applications of the text lie in equity, difference, and the recognition of racial, ethnic, and sexual diversity. Some of the issues discussed are of equity and fairness in observing young children, gender identities in the early years, and working with nontraditional families.

Helms, J. (2000). *A race is a nice thing to have: A guide to being a white person or understanding the white persons in your life*. Topeka, KS: Content Communications.

This book examines how the recognition of White racial identity may help to end racism. White people generally fail to understand that they have a racial identity and that having it does not have to be a negative. This book is useful for whites and others, and it includes examples and activities that enhance the reader's understanding of the part race plays in our lives.

Kalyanpur, M., & Harry, B. (1999). *Culture in special education: Building reciprocal family–professional relationships*. Baltimore: Paul H. Brookes Publishing Co.

This text is essential reading for future teachers, helping them become aware of traditional cultural stereotypes in special education. It explains how to cast these stereotypes aside in order to work more effectively with students' families.

Kendall, F.E. (2006). *Understanding white privilege: Creating pathways to authentic relationships across race*. Routledge: New York.

This book explores what it means to be white, how to talk about race and why it is important to understand white privilege. It shows how race frames experiences, relationships, and the way we see the world.

Mazel, E. (Ed.). (1998). *And don't call me a racist!* Lexington, MA: Argonaut Press.

This is a collection of more than 1,000 quotes from blacks and whites aimed at understanding and resolving the problems of prejudice and racism.

National Coalition Building Institute. (2003). *Principles into practice*. Washington, DC: Author.

This booklet offers examples of how leaders trained by the National Coalition Building Institute have helped their organizations and communities to combat all forms of racism and discrimination, make differences among groups a community asset, take principled and courageous stands, and fuel momentum for community change.

Peters, W. (1987). *A class divided: Then and now*. New Haven, CT: Yale University Press.

This book describes the 1985 reunion of students who were divided into blue- and brown-eyed groups for a lesson in discrimination and chronicles the profound and enduring effect on the students' lives and attitudes.

Van Ausdale, D., & Feagin, J. R. (2001). *The first R: How children learn race and racism*. Lanham, MD: Rowman and Littlefield Publishers.

This book is an account of how children as young as 3 years old learn about racial differences in the United States. A careful analysis of ethnographic data revealed that children were not too young to understand race and ethnicity and held a surprising array of racial attitudes, assumptions, and behaviors that they normally withhold from family members and other adults. The authors share implications for parents, teachers, and researchers.

Wagenheim, K., & Jimenez de Wagenheim, O. (Eds.). (2008). *The Puerto Ricans: A documentary history*. Princeton, NJ: Markus Wiener Publishers.

This collection covers 500 years of the people of Puerto Rico, including their political history, culture, unique identity, and relationship to the United States.

Web Resources

A Class Divided; http://www.pbs.org/wgbh/pages/frontline/shows/divided

This web site contains information on the program *A Class Divided*, which is about a public school teacher and her third-grade students, whom she divided into blue- and brown-eyed groups for a lesson in discrimination following the assassination of Dr. Martin Luther King, Jr. The site includes a discussion guide and other materials.

coAction Connection; http://www.antiracism.com

This organization provides diversity and communication training to schools and organizations with the philosophy that a communication structure that honors the presence of multiple perspectives can generate shared meaning and supports the development of trust.

Crosswalks Toolbox; http://www.fpg.unc.edu/~scpp/crosswalks/toolbox/index.cfm

This is an online source for teaching, training, and staff development. It describes resources for infusing cultural, linguistic, and ability diversity into preservice education.

National Latino Children's Institute; http://www.nlci.org

The National Latino Children's Institute (NLCI) is a nonprofit, nonpartisan organization that focuses on Latino children, with the mission to serve as the voice for young Latinos. NLCI promotes and implements the National Latino Children's Agenda through a variety of strategies.

Pew Hispanic Center; http://www.pewhispanic.org

The Pew Hispanic Center's mission is to improve understanding of the diverse Hispanic population in the United States and to chronicle Latinos' growing impact on the nation. The Center strives to inform debate on critical issues through dissemination of its research to policy makers, business leaders, academic institutions, and the media. A variety of reports are available to obtain information and statistics about the growing Hispanic population in the United States.

RACE: The Power of an Illusion; http://www.pbs.org/race/000_General/000_00-Home.htm

This is the online companion to California Newsreel's three-part documentary about race in society, science, and history. The web site provides informational readings, activities, and resources about race and the history of how race has been defined and has affected society.

Students Challenging Racism and (White) Privilege (SCRAP); http://www.canopyweb.com/racism

This web site has resources to increase awareness and understanding of racism, antiracism and whiteness. The materials on the web site do not take a colorblind or multicultural approach but one that approaches racism in relationship to power and privilege, explains how whites benefit from the disadvantages faced by people of color, and encourages groups to confront their involvement in systems of oppression. Many of the materials help to facilitate conversations and discussions to confront racism.

Walking the Walk: A Guide to Diversity Resources for Trainers; http://www.fpg.unc.edu/~walkingthewalk/pdfs/WTW_guide.pdf

This is an annotated listing of high-quality resources that can be used to grow or develop a more diverse and capable workforce to serve young children and their families. It is available free of charge.

Cross-Cultural Communication

Purpose

To understand different communication styles, foster positive cross-cultural interactions, and enhance communication with families and colleagues

Objectives

- Become familiar with different aspects of communication
- Develop skills for promoting successful communication between families and teachers or other service providers
- Develop skills for using interpreters when the provider does not speak the language spoken by the child and his or her family

Bueno cuando estás hablando y no miras a la persona a la cara, esto es considerado como falta de respeto. Sin embargo, en Puerto Rico no se da mucho énfasis en eso; si te miraron o no a los ojos, es igual. Y yo sé que en Latinoamérica los niños no le miran a la cara al maestro porque es más respeto mirar abajo. En Puerto Rico, la gente es más abierta, quiero decir más impulsiva; alguien te conoció ayer y ya hoy te saluda con un beso. El espacio es diferente; el americano necesita su espacio. En Puerto Rico, uno quiere ir a la casa de una amiga, tu vas y ya, tú llamas para ver si está y esto es para ahorrar el viaje, pero aquí tú no puedes ir a la casa de un americano sin llamar y ver cuando puedes ir.

Well, when you are talking and you don't look at the person's face, this is considered a lack of respect. However, in Puerto Rico, they don't place much emphasis on that. If they look you in the eye or don't, it's all the same. And I know that in Latin America the children don't look at the teacher's face, because it is more respectful to look down. In Puerto Rico, people are more open, meaning more impulsive; somebody met you yesterday and today they are already greeting you with a kiss. Space is different. The American needs his space. In Puerto Rico, you want to go to a friend's house, you go and you call to see if she is there, and this is to save a trip, but here you can't go to an American's house without calling to see when you can go.

—*Elizabeth, Puerto Rico*

For the purposes of communication, no one language is superior to another. Spanish is as good as English is as good as any indigenous language. Historically, certain language accents and dialects have been devalued, not because they are less efficient at conveying meaning but because they are often social class markers. (Pinker, 1994)

One of the responsibilities of early childhood professionals is to provide support to families. Together with families, professionals work to enhance and foster the development in the young children they serve. For effective practices to occur, there must be clear communication and positive interactions. When there is a language or cultural difference, successful communication can often become challenging. Professionals must understand aspects of cross-cultural communication, be able to foster positive cross-cultural interactions, and enhance their communication with families and their colleagues. For professionals working with children and families for whom English is not the first language, it is crucial to know how to work effectively with interpreters.

Primarily, humans use language to communicate. Language is a code in which we make specific symbols (words) stand for something else. Although the codes may be arbitrary (Why do we say "bird" to mean *bird*?), there are rules to govern how we make words, how we combine them, in what order and in what situation we use them (Reed, 2005). We begin to learn language from birth and will learn the forms and rules for whatever type of language (e.g., speech, sign language, communication symbols) we are exposed to. Virginia Satir (in Schwab, Baldwin, Gerber, Gomori, & Satir, 1989) commented on the importance of communication:

> Communication is to personal health, satisfactory interpersonal relationships, and productivity as breathing is to life. Effective communication can be both taught and learned. We were not born with the way we communicate. We learned it, mostly through modeling, in ways no one even knew or intended. (p. 128)

During the process of communication, messages are sent or delivered to another individual or group of individuals, and conversely, messages received from others are deciphered or interpreted for meaning. During communication, each individual seeks clarification in order to understand the meaning of the other's message, and the communicators take turns to make sure that the intent of their messages are clear and understood. This turn taking makes communication effective and successful.

Regardless of where they are born and reared, children who experience a typical development will learn the language of the community where they live in a particular sequence and at a similar pace. For example, from birth to 3 months, babies smile when a caregiver comes into view, make cooing sounds, and use a different cry to let the caregiver know if they are hungry or in pain. This is the earliest form of interaction. Table 2.1 presents a description of the developmental milestones in early language development as observed among most monolingual children. (See Module 4 for a discussion about language development among children growing up in bilingual environments.)

Table 2.1. Developmental milestones for language development

Age range	Expressive language	Receptive language
Newborn	Makes sounds to alert others of pleasure or pain	Listens to speech Startles or cries with unexpected or loud noises Quiets when hearing sound or voices
Birth to 3 months	Smiles at others Repeats the same sound a lot and "coos and goos" when content Uses a different cry for different situations, such as hunger and pain	Turns to others when they speak Smiles when hearing a caregiver's voice Appears to recognize familiar voices and quiets at the sound of those if crying Responds to comforting tones
4–6 months	Makes gurgling sounds or "vocal play" occur while playing with others or when occupying him- or herself happily Babbles so much that baby may sound as though he or she is "talking" Babbles in a speech-like manner that includes many sounds, such as the bilabial (two lip) sounds /p/, /b/, and /m/ Can tell others, by using sounds or gestures, when something is wanted Can make very urgent noises to prompt others into action	Responds to changes in tone of voice, to sounds other than speech (e.g., toys that make sounds, music) Pays attention to the source of various new sounds in the environment
7–12 months	Changes sound of babbling to include more consonants and long and short vowels Uses speech or other sounds (i.e., other than crying) in order to get and hold others' attention Speaks first words (although probably not very clearly), such as "MaMa," "Doggie," "Night Night," "Bye Bye"	Obviously listens when spoken to, turns and looks at the speaker's face when called by name Enjoys simple games and finger play Recognizes the names of familiar objects and people (e.g., "Mommy," "car," "eyes," "phone," "key") Begins to respond to requests (e.g., "Give it to Nana") and questions (e.g., "More juice?")
1–2 years	Accumulates more words as each month passes Will ask two-word questions, such as "Where ball?" "What's that?" "More juice?" and "What that?" Combines two words in other ways to make sentences, such as "Birdie go," "No doggie," and "More push" Uses more initial consonants; words become clearer	Points to pictures in a book when named Can point to a few body parts when asked Can follow simple commands (e.g., "Push the ball!") and understand simple questions (e.g., "Where's the kitty?") Likes listening to simple stories Enjoys it when others sing songs or say rhymes
2–3 years	Seems to have a word for almost everything. Utterances are usually one, two, or three words long, and family members can usually understand them May ask for, or draw attention to, something by naming it (e.g., "Elephant"), saying one of its attributes ("Big!"), or commenting ("Wow!").	Understands two-stage commands (e.g., "Get your shoes and put them in the basket") and contrasting concepts or meanings such as *hot/cold, stop/go, in/out,* and *nice/yucky.* Notices sounds like the telephone or doorbell ringing and may point or become excited, get someone to answer, or attempt to answer him- or herself
3–4 years	Combines four or more words to make longer sentences Talks about things that have happened away from home Wants to talk about preschool, friends, outings, and interesting experiences Usually speaks fluently and clearly, and people outside of the family can understand most communications	Understands simple "Who?" "What?" and "Where?" questions Can hear others when they call from another room
4–5 years	Speaks clearly and fluently in an easy-to-listen-to voice Can construct long and detailed sentences (e.g., "We went to the zoo, but we had to come home early because Josie wasn't feeling well") Can tell a long and involved story by sticking to the topic and using "adult-like" grammar Pronounces most sounds correctly but still has difficulty with /r/, /v/, and /th/ Can communicate easily with familiar adults and with other children May tell fantastic "tall tales" and engage strangers in conversation	Enjoys stories and can answer simple questions about them Hears and understands nearly everything that is said to him or her at home, preschool, or child care

Source: Bowen (1998).

Culture and Communication

Sus hijos, los de mi hermana . . . son muy fríos; a veces saludan, a veces no te saludan . . . Aquí no lo hacen, que besitos ni que besitos. Aquí ni te dan la mano, por no contagiarse con los microbios. Aquí son tan meticulosos; nosotros somos diferentes. Yo quiero que mi hija tenga la forma cálida de ser, como lo somos los latinos: cariñosa, educada.

Her children, my sister's children . . . are very cold [emotionally]; sometimes they greet you, sometimes they don't greet you . . . Living here, they don't greet you with a kiss. Here [in the United States], they don't even shake your hand because they are afraid of catching germs. Here they are very meticulous; we are different. I want my daughter to be warm [emotionally], as we Latinos are: loving, well mannered.

—Dora, Argentina

How does culture affect communication? In addition to learning the vocabulary and grammar of a particular language, the cultural rules of social interaction must be learned as well. Children closely monitor the conversations between their siblings and adult family members and learn when to join in, how to respond appropriately, how to take turns, and so forth. By age 4, most typically developing children know how to adjust their speech to fit the age, sex, and social status of their listener (Berk, 2002). People develop a set of expectations and rules about communicating with others at a very early age. These expectations and rules (often unstated) are influenced by the culture of the community.

Indeed, all facets of human life are influenced by culture, including child-rearing practices, food preferences, help-seeking behavior, and communication styles. A commonly cited example of the way culture affects communication is the different communicative styles of males and females. In the book, *Men Are from Mars, Women Are from Venus* (Gray, 1992) the author proposes metaphorically that previously Martians and Venusians had happy relationships because they respected and accepted each other's differences. However, they (men and women) developed amnesia after coming to earth, and they forgot that they were from different planets and were supposed to be different. Gray provided guidance on how men and women should interpret each other's language, determine its meaning, and communicate effectively with one another. Whether one agrees with Gray's analysis and assignment of gender communication styles, the point is that effective communication skills are critically important in developing and maintaining positive personal and professional relationships. Gray was proposing that in general, the cultures of women and men differ. It is important to note that Gray's book did not address gender relationships across cultures. However, the way in which women and men relate to each other is influenced by their cultural heritage. Behavioral differences in the genders are learned and not determined by physiology; behavior that is considered masculine in one culture may be considered feminine in another. These factors are also guided by where the individuals grew up (e.g., in a rural community or an urban community), their educational level, and their socioeconomic status.

Misunderstandings can occur among individuals who share the same cultural heritage. However, it is more likely that miscommunication and misunderstanding will occur when individuals have different cultural backgrounds or speak different languages because their communication styles and language forms are governed by different rules.

Creating positive interactions with others requires a person to become aware of his or her own preferred communicative style and to become knowledgeable about the multiple aspects of communication. When professionals and families learn to communicate effectively with one another, they are able to work in partnership to support children's development.

Verbal and Nonverbal Communication

Primero y número uno, no tocar a la gente, y nosotros sí tocamos. Número dos: hay señales que tú no puedes hacer. Yo me cuido mucho. Yo muevo mucho las manos cuando hablo. Ahora me cuido porque a los seis meses que había entrado, alguien me acusó que le estaba haciendo un gesto rudo, y no es que era un gesto rudo; lo que pasa es que manejo las manos mucho cuando hablo español.

First and foremost, don't touch people, and we do touch. Number two: there are gestures that you can't make. I am very careful. I move my hands a lot when I talk. Now I am careful because six months after I came, somebody accused me of making a rude gesture, and it wasn't that it was a rude gesture. What happens is that I move my hands a lot when I speak Spanish.

—Cristina, El Salvador

Verbal Communication

It is essential to consider both verbal and nonverbal aspects of communication in order to achieve effective communication. Verbal communication involves the use of speech to exchange ideas or convey information. Most aspects of verbal communication (e.g., tone, volume, rate of speech, accent) are acquired at an early age and are greatly influenced by what is appropriate in a particular family or community. Thus, the interpretation of tone of voice, volume, and speed is based on personal experience and may be influenced by bias, stereotypes, and/or prejudice. Children learn the acceptable tone of voice to use when responding to their parents or other adults. Certain tones are interpreted as disrespectful. In addition, some words are considered disrespectful, regardless of the tone. Suppose a child is outside playing and hears his or her mother calling. If the child answers with "What?" instead of "Yes, Mama," the child's mother may not be happy. Or, in a culture where the "inside voice" is quiet, what happens when someone uses the "outside voice" inside? Is that person angry, or is he or she being rude?

Individuals residing in the United States who learn English as a second language are often told that they speak with an accent. However, everyone speaks with an accent. As the American Speech-Language-Hearing Association (ASHA) points out, "Accents are a natural part of spoken languages. It is important to realize that no accent is better than another. It should also be stressed that accents are not a speech or language disorder" (ASHA, n.d.; Reed, 2005). Many people take pride in their accents; however, when communication becomes difficult or when individuals feel that their accents interfere with their self-esteem, their career, or their ability to lead a happy and productive life, they may turn to a speech-language pathologist for therapy to reduce or modify their accent. Paying more attention to how someone speaks rather than to what he or she says may cause difficulties in communicating. For example, what kind of message do you get when someone speaks to you in a very loud or soft voice? What do you think when someone speaks with a Northern accent, or a Southern accent, or a "foreign" accent? How do you respond?

Bueno, hay uso de palabras diferentes, según de donde vengan. Para algunas personas, algunas palabras tienen diferente significados. Pienso que los latinos somos más expresivos. . . . Especialmente nuestro tono de voz es mucho más alto que el de aquí. Eso siempre me ha llamado la atención, incluso con las relaciones con mi marido. Ay, el me dice, '¿Por qué gritas?' Y yo le digo, 'No es que estoy gritando, es como yo hablo.' Pero es que cuando tengo que explicar algo que para mi es importante o que llame la atención subo el tono de mi voz.

Well, there are different word usages, according to where they come from. For some people, some words have different meanings. I think that Latinos are more expressive. . . . especially our tone of voice is higher. I have always noticed this, including with my husband. He says to me, "Why are you shouting?" and I tell him, "It's not that I'm shouting, it's how I speak." When I have to explain something that is very important to me or to get somebody's attention, I raise my voice.

—*Maria, Mexico*

Nonverbal Communication

Some people are not aware that they communicate and send many messages without actually speaking. They may make decisions based on a "feeling" that they got during an interaction. Nonverbal communication is powerful and includes body language, posture, facial expression, eye contact, space, and proximity. As children acquire the rules of communication related to their culture, they may learn that it is disrespectful to look at the eyes of an adult or person of authority. When a teacher tells a child, "Look at me when I'm talking," he or she likely means, "This lets me know that you are paying attention to me." However, if this child has been taught not to look at an adult's eyes (i.e., the child's parents taught him or her that this is

Imagine the "dance" of advance and retreat between two people whose preferences for proximity are not matched.

disrespectful or challenging to an authority figure), the child is in an obviously confusing situation. The child is getting conflicting instructions, as the same action can bring both praise and disapproval. What should the child do?

A common source of trepidation in cross-cultural communication is figuring out the amount of distance that is comfortable between two individuals. People in the United States are accustomed to having their space, even if they are not aware of it. The phrases "too close for comfort" and "in your face" imply that someone has moved into or beyond the place that is comfortable. Imagine the "dance" of advance and retreat between two people whose preferences for proximity are not matched. As one person moves forward, the other steps back; as one person moves back, the other steps forward. In *The Silent Language*, Edward Hall (1981b), speaking about the interaction distance in Latin America, stated,

> Indeed, people cannot talk comfortably with one another unless they are very close to the distance that evokes either sexual or hostile feelings in the North American. . . . They think we are distant or cold, withdrawn and unfriendly. . . . We . . . are constantly accusing them of breathing down our necks, crowding us, and spraying our faces.

Are you aware of your own use of nonverbal communication? Does it make you uncomfortable to stand or sit very close to others? Do you unconsciously use your desk or other furniture as a barricade to create space between you and others? Do you like it when people look you in the eye? What does it mean when people fold their arms across their body? Cross their legs? Table 2.2 provides information about differing ways of interpreting such behavior.

Mi familia habla durísimo. Ahora me molesta cuando voy a Santo Domingo; llego a la casa de mis papás (yo digo la casa de locos), y las niñas se molestan porque no están acostumbradas, y tú te das cuenta de cosas que no te dabas cuenta porque tu vivías en ese ambiente. Yo por lo menos trato de ser considerada, de no hablar duro.

My family speaks so loudly. Now it annoys me when I go to Santo Domingo. I come to my parents' house (I call it the "crazy house"), and the girls get annoyed because they aren't accustomed [to it]. You realize things that you didn't use to realize because you lived in that environment. I at least try to be considerate, not to speak loudly.

—*Jocelyn, Dominican Republic*

Table 2.2. Different interpretations of the same behavior

Direct eye contact means that you are trustworthy, interested, and respectful.	Direct eye contact means that you are challenging authority, disrespectful, and inviting intimacy.
Smiling means that you are friendly, comfortable, and pleased with the interaction.	Smiling means that you are nervous, uncomfortable, or embarrassed.
Sharing personal information is unprofessional, an undue distraction, and a waste of time.	Sharing personal stories helps to establish rapport and develops a cordial and reciprocal relationship for future work.

High and Low Cultural Context Encounters

High context: *A more implicit communication style; primary emphasis is on the multiple nonverbal features of communication, such as facial expressions, use of silence, and body language*

Low context: *A more explicit communication style; primary emphasis is on verbal skills such as expression, debate, and consultation*

Source: Gudykunst (2003).

Many cultural experts categorize basic styles of communication into either a high or low cultural context (Chen, Chan, & Brekken, 2000; Hall, 1981a). Hall (1981a) described how context is used to filter information. When there are many different things happening in the environment, the amount of information that one pays attention to determines whether one is operating in a low or high context.

In high cultural context encounters, more attention is given to the circumstances of the interaction. Individuals tend to pay attention to multiple features, such as facial expressions, use of silence, body language, or vocal utterances ("Uh huh"). A great deal of meaning is conveyed implicitly. In fact, sometimes the most important aspect of the interaction is not what one actually says but what is left unsaid. Mothers often communicate approval or warning to their children with a mere look or glance. When the children see this "mother look," they may interpret it to mean, "Stop what you are doing right now"; if they persist in the behavior, the next look may mean, "Just wait until I get you home."

In low cultural context encounters, the attention is much more focused on what is actually spoken. There is an emphasis on the ability to express oneself verbally. The use of discussion, debate, conversation, and consultation is frequent in most interactions, whether at school or work, and in relationships. There is an expectation that everyone in the environment will contribute to the discussions. Lack of verbal interaction in this sense can be interpreted as disinterest, ignorance, or inattention.

It is difficult to classify specific cultures into either high or low context, and it is more accurate to say that there is a continuum with a lot of variation. For example, Western cultures are most often considered to be low context, with communication being more explicit; however, there are many factors that may influence communication styles. The level of acculturation—that is, the extent to which individuals have borrowed traits or adapted or modified their cultural characteristics as a result of prolonged contact with the new culture (National Center for Cultural Competence, 2004)—results in a wide continuum of communication styles. Other influences or factors include the amount of time spent in the new environment, the age at which an individual left his or her home country, educational level, and socioeconomic status. Culture has a powerful influence on communication style, but awareness of other influences that contribute to an individual's style of communication helps to avoid stereotypes. The uniqueness of each individual and of each family makes it impossible to characterize the individual's or family's communication style based on cultural or ethnic group identification alone.

Developing Listening Skills

When you understand how a particular family prefers to communicate, you get a sense of the communicative environment in which the family lives; thus, you can work more effectively with the child. Receiving and accurately understanding someone's message involves paying attention to the nonverbal behaviors of the sender and actively listening to what he or she has to say.

To be prepared to work with a child and his or her family, you first need to be aware of your own style and preferences for communicating by asking yourself questions such as

- What biases, if any, do I have about the different ways people communicate?

- How do I react to the accent or speaking style of a particular family or cultural group?

- What specific strengths can I, as a professional, bring to the interaction?

- How can I improve my communication?

Next, it is important learn about the family and their preferred mode of communication. Many times the style of communication is unconscious; the preferred mode may not be articulated. How can you find out about a family's communication preferences?

- Listen to what the family says and watch for cues.

- Do not assume that you understand nonverbal cues; ask questions.

- Observe interactions between family members.

- Ask permission to address sensitive topics.

- Read information about the family's ethnic or cultural group to understand its history in the community.

- Be aware of differences in perceived power relationships.

When interacting with the family, attention needs to be given to your nonverbal behaviors. It is important to be comfortable and relaxed, to lean forward slightly, and to be aware of personal distance. It is important to be attentive to the amount of eye contact that feels comfortable with each family and to be aware of your own body posture and gestures. For example, when you nod your head up and down, does this mean that you understand, that you are listening, or that you agree? Avoid distracting gestures, fidgeting, or interrupting the person who is speaking. Show the speaker that you are listening by using facial expressions that are empathetic by and using minimal verbal encouragers (e.g., "Mm-hmm," "Yes, go on") at appropriate times during the interaction.

Most important, it is the ultimate responsibility of you—the professional who works with children and families—to establish and maintain effective communication. It is a responsibility that comes with the job. When professionals aim to support families' abilities to enhance and foster the development of their children, everyone wins. They can be successful in this aim by creating an atmosphere in which parents feel that they are equal members of the team; are comfortable communicating their wishes, desires, and priorities for their children; and are willing and able to work together for the sake of the children. Working in partnership with the family, the professional can gain a sense of the communicative environment in which the child lives and be able to more effectively work with the child.

Because first impressions are lasting, good communication begins with the first telephone call, the first knock on the door, or the first encounter. It is a good idea to ask yourself this: During my first interaction with a family, do I make sure to ask them what they want and how they prefer to receive information?

Some Strategies for Active Listening[1]

Active listening is an important tool for effective communication. Active listening involves using open questions, which can be directive yet encourage talking; using paraphrasing to slow down the conversational flow and focus the conversation; exploring feelings related to the encounter before beginning to problem solve; and summarizing to help wrap up and bring the conversation to a close.

Asking Open Questions

Closed questions are often associated with those questions posed to someone on the witness stand or someone being interrogated. These are those questions that get straight to the point—"Yes" or "No," without elaboration, as if one were in court, in the witness box, being questioned by an opposing attorney. Such questions usually garner one-word answers, and nothing more. Actively listening requires using questions that require more than a "Yes" or "No" answer and that implicitly say to the family, "Tell me more." This type of question helps to gain relevant information in order to better meet the needs of the children and their families. Here are some tips on asking open questions:

1. Begin questions with "How" or "What," as opposed to "Why." Using "How "and "What" gains information, but using "Why" sounds more accusatory.

2. Use questions to clarify, elaborate feelings, and problem solve (e.g., "How do you feel about that?" "What have you already tried?" "How did that work?").

3. Keep questions clear and simple.

Paraphrasing

Paraphrasing is restating what the person said using other words. An accurate paraphrase helps the person feel listened to and understood. Paraphrasing is not making interpretations about the meanings behind the other person's statements.

1. Be brief when paraphrasing.

2. Try to state the essence of what the person said.

---

[1]*Source:* D'Andrea and Salovey (1996).

3. Check perceptions. Get the person's reactions to your paraphrase to ensure that you are accurate. For instance, you might say, "So what you are saying is you were very upset when Johnny came home wet because you feel that we are not paying enough attention to him to know when he has to use the potty," or "Let me see if I understand this right: When Johnny came home from school wet, it made you feel that we are not paying enough attention to him, and that upsets you."

Exploring Feelings

Although your role may not involve being a counselor, you will be dealing with your own feelings as well as the feelings of the families that you work with. Ignoring the feelings that are involved will not build a successful working relationship. Families may feel that they need someone who cares and can share in their successes and challenges. Unacknowledged or unresolved feelings can become an obstacle to developing options and making decisions about the best recourse to take. When you suspect that there may be concerns, it is important to listen, provide support or a referral, and wait until the family is ready to make decisions about options.

1. Identify the feelings through questions, and paraphrase spoken feelings. This helps to clarify for people what they are expressing. You might say, "How does that make you feel?" "What feelings does that bring up in you?" or "So, what I heard you say is that you are very frustrated."

2. Reflect unspoken feelings. Do not make assumptions about the person's behavior or mannerisms. Instead, say something like "You appear to be tense" or "You seem nervous."

3. Define and clarify feelings. Avoid interpreting what the person means by a particular term. An example might be asking, "What are you feeling when you say that you are depressed?"

4. Acknowledge and validate the feelings. For instance, you might say, "That must be very frustrating" or "Being a new mom can be so difficult."

Summarizing

Summarizing helps bring the conversation to a close and states the next steps—for example, "I'll send you the information on toilet training that we discussed. Please let me know what the doctor recommends, after you have seen her." Summarizing is also good for shifting the conversation to a different topic. Keep the following summarizing tips in mind:

1. Simply use a larger paraphrase to restate and capture the essence of everything discussed in the conversation.

2. Put the conversation into a logical and usable order.

3. Keep it brief and check perceptions (e.g., ask, "Is that right?").

Interpretation and Translation Services

Entonces, claramente lo que hago cuando viene una abreviación, tengo que decir lo que significa que. El hecho de que los veo semanalmente muchos de estos clientes me da también la oportunidad de saber que significa "no entiendo" con un gesto, una expresión de la cara. Eso me alcanza para saber que realmente hay que aclararlo. . . . Lo que hago primero: les digo en inglés lo que voy a decir en español, como clarificación, como obteniendo la aprobación. En otras palabras, no dejo a nadie descontado. No tomo por parte mía un rol que no es. En otras palabras, yo no puedo cambiar las palabras que alguien dice. Esas son sus palabras, yo soy solamente una voz. . . . No hay forma de rectificar una mala noticia; también entiendo que la forma de los americanos que se expresan es un poco engañosa. Ellos no quieren hacer lucirlo tan malo como es, y las palabras uno traduce literalmente cuando viene; una mala noticia puede sonar menos mala noticia de lo que realmente es. . . . En otras palabras, a veces los ornamentos, en la parte médica, pienso que se deben quitar en muchos aspectos. . . . Yo he hablado con los doctores en ese aspecto y les he pedido que, cuando las noticias no son importantes, que por favor sean más directos.

So, clearly, what I do when an abbreviation comes up, I have to say what stands for what. . . . The fact that I see many of these clients weekly gives me the opportunity to know what gesture or facial expression means "I don't understand." This helps me to know that they need clarification. . . . First, I tell [the person I am interpreting for] in English what I am going to say in Spanish, as clarification, like obtaining approval. In other words, I don't leave anybody out. I don't take a role that isn't mine. In other words, I can't change the words that somebody says. Those are their words; I am only a voice. . . . There is no way to rectify bad news. I also understand that the American way of expression is a little misleading. They don't want to make it seem as bad as it is, and one translates the words literally as they come; bad news can sound better than it actually is. . . . In other words, sometimes I think that in many respects they should get rid of the ornaments in the medical report. . . . I have spoken with the doctors about this and I have asked that, when the news isn't important, that they please be more direct.

—Leonor, Paraguay

In an ideal world, families would work with service providers who are from similar backgrounds, speak the same language, and are able to adequately communicate with and understand each other. However, there are approximately 6,000 different languages in the world, and 330 of them are used in the United States. The number and percentage of people in the United States who spoke a language other than English at home increased between 1990 and 2000. In 2000, 18% of the total population age 5 and older, or 47 million people, reported they spoke a language other than English at home. These figures were up from 14% (31.8 million) in 1990 and 11% (23.1 million) in 1980. The number of people who spoke a language other than English at home grew by 38% in the 1980s and by 47% in the 1990s. Although the population age 5 and older grew by one fourth from 1980 to 2000, the number who spoke a language other than English at home more than doubled (Shin & Bruno, 2003). Second-generation children once were encouraged to adopt the customs, culture, and language of the majority culture where they resided. With the early 21st century's greater recognition and celebration of cultural differences, however, people are more likely to maintain and share their primary language with their children and to promote bilingualism as a reflection of ethnic pride and identity (Reed, 2005).

Because the United States is made up of diverse individuals, it has become critically important to have access to and be able to use interpreters to assist with communication. Although there are mechanical means of interpretation, the only reliable—and, ultimately, the fastest—translator is a human being who is deeply conversant in the languages and the subject matter (Hall, 1981b).

What Is an Interpreter?

An *interpreter* converts the content of one language into another language through speech or sign language.

A *translator* converts the content from one language to another language in writing.

Sometimes the words *interpreter* and *translator* are used interchangeably; however, the two terms do not have the same meaning. An interpreter converts one language into another through speech or sign language. A translator usually does this conversion in writing. Interpreters perform two common roles in early care, education, and early intervention. First, they act as providers of information by changing the words from one language to another. Second, they are cultural mediators who not only interpret the words but also facilitate cross-cultural understanding and communication. In early intervention, an interpreter is an equal member of the interdisciplinary team. Most U.S. early intervention systems have developed specific training programs for working with interpreters and provide an orientation to help interpreters understand the purpose, process, and terminology of their particular system of care, services, or supports.

Methods of Interpretation

There are three major methods of interpretation:

1. Consecutive interpretation involves changing the message from one language to another after speaker's pauses. This is commonly used in home visits and in meetings with families.

2. Simultaneous interpretation involves interpreting at the same time that the message is heard. Headphones are often used for this process. This type of interpretation is used in large gatherings such as at United Nations meetings. Interpreting sign language into spoken English is another example of simultaneous interpretation.

3. Narrative interpretation involves describing the general topic of conversation or explaining the immediate context or situation to an onlooker.

What to Look for in an Interpreter

Sí hay traductores, y como le comenté a Pamela, "Oye, Pamela, siempre que voy al hospital y pido un traductor, él se pone hablar como si fuera el doctor." Y ahí están cuando ellos deberían decirme lo que el doctor les está diciendo, pero yo sí miro todo eso y ¿a quién se lo digo? ¿A quién le digo, "Mira, está pasando esto"? cuando en realidad no sabemos con quién dirigirnos ni explicarles en el hospital. Pero a veces ni los traductores saben lo que te están diciendo. . . . Y la verdad que sí entiendo. A veces no necesito un traductor; el único problema es hablar más claro.

There are translators, and as I commented to Pamela, "Whenever I go to the hospital and ask for a translator, he starts talking as if he were the doctor." And here they are when they should be telling me what the doctor is saying. I do see all of this. Whom should I tell? Whom should I tell, "Look, this is going on," when in reality we don't know whom to address or how to explain it in the hospital? But sometimes the translators don't know what they are telling you, either. . . . And the truth is that I do understand. Sometimes I don't need a translator; the only problem is to speak more clearly.

—*Juana, Mexico*

Being bilingual does not mean that a person will make a good interpreter. Ideally, an interpreter has participated in formal interpreter training, is proficient in the languages of both parties, and is experienced in cross-cultural communication. Such an interpreter understands the respective cultures, including the subtle nuances of each. A good interpreter needs to have

- Excellent interpersonal skills

- The ability to be sensitive to the feelings of all participants

- The ability to understand the nuances of each participant's intended meanings

- The ability to set aside emotions and opinions while interpreting

Interpreters working in the early intervention or special education field need to have basic understanding of the service system and the terminology that is to be used for each interaction. When using an interpreter for the first time, the program should make sure that the interpreter understands the way a particular program operates and the relevant terminology that is going to be used. Creating a glossary of terms and sharing this with the interpreter beforehand will help ensure that the information is interpreted accurately. Note that for certain technical terms, a direct translation may not exist and the interpreter needs to determine how best to convey this information. It can be a bit disconcerting to the parties involved to discover that an interpreted message appears to be twice as long. It may in fact take many more or far fewer words to convey the same meaning in different languages.

Some states have enacted legislation that bans the use of children as interpreters in health care institutions (Angelelli, 2004). There are many reasons why it is not considered good practice to use children within the family as interpreters. Although a child may be bilingual or have a better command of both languages than the parents or the provider, the child may not have the maturity to understand the concepts being discussed or the words to convey them. Using a child as interpreter can upset the dynamics within a family by putting the parents in a position of vulnerability. Using a child to interpret places the burden of adult responsibility on a child—that is, it forces the child to deal with a situation that should be handled by adults. Using children as interpreters creates an unusual amount of stress for the child and the family and should be avoided under all circumstances.

When selecting an interpreter, one needs to be sensitive to issues of age and gender—of both the interpreter and the participating family members. For instance, in some families, it may be taboo to discuss certain personal issues with a member of the opposite sex. In addition, make sure that the interpreter understands the specific dialect of the person for whom he or she will be interpreting.

Models of Interpreter Services

Businesses and health care institutions have acquired a lot of experience using interpreters. The National Center on Cultural Competence, the Cross-Cultural Health Care Program, and Diversity Rx are three programs that provide useful information on models and strategies for overcoming linguistic and cultural barriers to health care and mental health equity. Each program must determine the model that works best for it by considering the variety of language groups that it serves, the number of families who require interpretation, the availability of professional interpreters, the degree of commitment to quality, and cost restraints. The common approaches for providing services to different language groups range from no interpreter at all—which is an unacceptable approach (not to mention a violation of current law)—to a program that has bilingual providers. Between these opposite points are other options that may be considered. The most promising models currently include the following.

- *Professional on-site interpreters:* This model involves hiring or contracting with professionally trained interpreters on a full-time or part-time basis. This model also involves contracting with language agencies that provide interpreters or using interpreters provided through voluntary language banks.

- *Volunteer interpreters:* This can be an excellent resource for interpretation, but having a volunteer from the community necessitates developing safeguards to ensure privacy and confidentiality and avoid gossip or difficulties in social relationships. In addition, caution must be exercised when using interpreters from volunteer programs because some programs may not compel volunteers to meet the training, standards, and quality levels that a service provider requires for interpreters.

- *Remote interpreting (in-house):* In this method, an agency or other facility selects and hires a number of interpreters and houses them in a central location to make the most efficient use of their time. The provider and family members are equipped with two headsets or two handsets and are connected by telephone with the interpreter. The interpretation is done simultaneously over the telephone. Several medical centers in the United States are experimenting with this model.

- *Telephonic interpreting (contracted):* This approach involves using a language line operated by a commercial company. Agencies register to gain access to an interpreter over the telephone on demand. Language line interpreters are usually expected to cover calls on multiple topics: legal, insurance, medical, finance, or tourism. Few interpreters can be competent in all topics; therefore, it is important to ask questions about the selection process to ensure high-quality interpretation for specific needs. This service may be very useful in an emergency or for an unplanned event, in a situation for which the conversation would naturally take place over the telephone, or when there is a need for a language that is not common in the location.

Strategies that Promote Effective Communication During Interpretation

No quiero ser una barrera entre el terapista y el cliente; esa es mi idea. Pero he visto intérpretes que interpretan y ponen de su cosecha y se meten en la terapia y opinan. Entonces ya no eres un intérprete; ya eres parte de la terapia. El rol debe estar muy definido.

I do not want to be a barrier between the therapist and the client; this is my idea. But I have seen interpreters that interpret and make it their own and they meddle in the therapy and give their opinion. Then you aren't an interpreter; you are now part of the therapy. The role should be well-defined.

—Claudia, Colombia

The interpreter and the provider work together as a team during the interaction with the family to communicate needed information. Preparation is the key to having a successful encounter when using an interpreter. Unless it is an emergency, it is not proper or fair to pull someone in 5 minutes before a meeting and ask him or her to act as an interpreter. The provider (whether teacher, early interventionist, therapist, or physician) should schedule a time to meet with the interpreter ahead of time. During this meeting, it is important to share the purpose and expected outcomes of the interaction, the name and role of the participants, the expected role of the interpreter, and relevant terminology. This meeting provides an opportunity to establish a rapport and answer questions about your work together. The service provider should share information about the family's background and any issues of concern.

The seating arrangement in the room contributes to making the interaction successful (see Figure 2.1). The seats should be arranged in a triangle, with the provider sitting directly in front of the family member and the interpreter to the side. At the beginning of the interaction with the family, the provider should make sure the family understands the role of the interpreter and that the purpose of the interpretation process is communication and enhanced understanding. The provider should explain to family participants that at any time, they can stop the interpreter to ask for clarification or repetition and can even request a different interpreter. For example, individuals from different regions may not speak the same dialect, and the

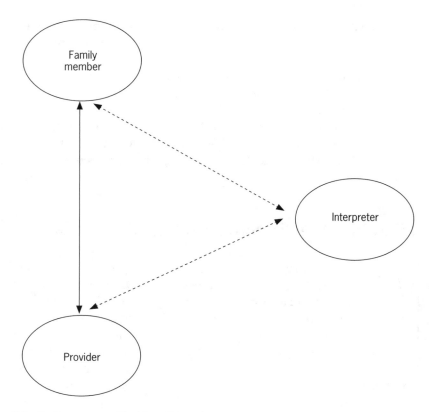

Figure 2.1. Seating arrangement for interpreting session.

words used in one dialect may not make sense or have the same meaning in another. In addition, individuals who come from the same country may in fact speak different languages; as cited in Module 1, not all Latinos speak Spanish. From the start, the provider should be sure to look at the family member when speaking, not at the interpreter. Note that during interpretation, the interpreter speaks in the first person and not for him- or herself. For example, if the provider says, "Mrs. Hernandez, tell me what Pablo likes to eat in the morning," the interpreter should interpret "Mrs. Hernandez, tell me what Pablo likes to eat in the morning" and not "She [meaning the provider] wants to know what Pablo likes to eat in the morning." A good time to discuss this is in the premeeting with the interpreter. Table 2.3 provides a summary of guidelines for a good interpretation session.

After the encounter, the interpreter and the provider should meet to debrief the meeting. This debriefing meeting provides an opportunity for the provider and the interpreter to talk about how things went. Did they speak slowly enough? Does the interpreter believe that the family understood everything? Were there some terms that were confusing or needed more explanation? Would it be helpful to have a dictionary or diagrams? Should there be a telephone call to follow up? What should they do next time to improve the interaction? Although it is important for the interpreter to remain neutral while interpreting, he or she may have important information to share with the provider during the debriefing meeting.

Table 2.3. Guidelines for good interpreting

Service provider	Interpreter	Family
Use jargon-free communication.	Address and respect the family's feelings about sharing personal information.	Use simple statements and questions.
Explain acronyms and avoid colloquialisms.	Maintain neutrality and confidentiality.	Speak slowly and clearly.
Use simple statements and questions.	Ask for explanations of acronyms or professional jargon if they are used.	Ask questions to clarify points if you do not understand or feel that you are not being understood.
Speak slowly and clearly but not loudly.	If needed, ask participants to speak or sign more slowly and to stop side conversations.	If you do not understand the interpreter, stop the meeting and request another interpreter or reschedule for another time with a different interpreter.
Listen without judgment.		
Be aware of nonverbal behaviors.		
Make time for communication.		
Attend to the interaction and avoid side conversations.		
Emphasize confidentiality.		
Verify purpose and roles in the meeting.		
Address family members directly—do not only look at the interpreter.		

Source: Moore, Perez-Mendez, Beatty, and Eiserman (1999).

One thing that I know is parents. They usually will tell me that they know by the teacher's expression and all her gestures how the teacher is feeling, even when you're interpreting while the teacher is talking. They may not know the words, but they know that she is irritated with something or she is happy about something or they can sense all that. . . . [It] is very hard to stay very neutral in these things to me, especially being a teacher and knowing, you know.

—Patricia, Cuba

Beware of Translation Software!

Some programs have begun to use translation software to assist them in providing materials to their families in their native language. Current software programs cannot adequately substitute for having a human translate written documents. However, these programs can be used, with caution, in an emergency when there is no alternative. To ensure the desired result, first translate the document into the language that is needed (e.g., Spanish); next, take the translated document and translate it back into English. Compare the original with the translated English version. To illustrate how this software works, this book's authors used translation software to translate a parent tip sheet into Spanish. The Spanish translation was then translated back into English. Figure 2.2 shows the resulting English translation; Figure 2.3 shows the actual wording from the original source.

Tops of Security

For babies:

- your child should always be in a seat of infantile car that confronts reverse well held in the seat of behind when in a car or taxi.
- Juguetes should be simple and unbreakable without pieces.
- they Always place his baby in his back when he goes to sleep to reduce the risk of Syndrome of crib death (SIDS).
- Exhibition to the smoke of cigarette is bad for the health of his child.
- they never leave his baby in peace in a bed or table; she can roll rapidly far!
- they never retire to his baby neglected in a sink or tub of the water.
- Verify his house for risks of accident, poisons, medicines, sharp objects, and rims of table.
- Them Are careful handling his baby. It is dangerous for him to be shaken or shaken.
- plastic lids of plug Use them in electrical captures.

Figure 2.2. For illustration only: Results after this book's authors used translation software to translate a parent tip sheet into Spanish and then back into English. (*Source:* Connecticut Birth to Three, n.d.)

Safety Tips

For babies:

- Your infant should always be in a rear-facing infant car seat securely fastened in the back seat when in a car or taxi.
- Toys should be simple and unbreakable with no small parts.
- Always place your baby on his back when he goes to sleep to reduce the risk of Sudden Infant Death Syndrome (SIDS).
- Exposure to cigarette smoke is bad for your infant's health.
- Never leave your baby alone on a bed or table; she may quickly roll off!
- Never leave your baby unattended in a sink or tub of water.
- Check your home for accident hazards, poisons, medicines, sharp objects, and table edges.
- Be careful when handling your baby. It is dangerous for him to be jerked or shaken.
- Use plastic plug covers on electrical outlets.

Figure 2.3. Original text of the safety tip sheet cited in Figure 2.2. (From Connecticut Birth to Three. [n.d.]. *Safety tips*. Retrieved March 4, 2010, from http://www.birth23.org/Families/SafetyTips.asp; reprinted by permission.)

Conclusion

The intention of Module 2 has been to familiarize professionals with different aspects of communication and explain the impact of culture on the styles of communicating. The module noted the importance of fostering positive cross-cultural interactions and enhancing communication between families and providers and among colleagues. On a related note, it presented ways to develop skills for using interpreters when the provider does not speak the same language as the child and family.

Ayuda muchísimo, porque hay momentos en que uno no entiende nada de lo que ellos dicen. Ahora de repente entiendo más inglés, pero antes yo me trancaba, y ellos para mí eran tan importante. Y necesito el intérprete porque hay palabras que ellos me dicen y yo no entiendo y empiezo a preguntar, "¿Qué es eso? ¿Para qué es eso?" Y muchas preguntas más.

It helps so much, because there are moments when one doesn't understand anything that they say. Now maybe I understand more English, but before there was a barrier, and they were so important for me. And I need the interpreter because there are words that they say to me and I don't understand and I start to ask, "What is this? What is this for?" And many more questions.

—*Mariana, Mexico*

Key Ideas to Remember

- In addition to learning the vocabulary and grammar of a language, the rules of social interaction which are governed by culture must be learned as well.

- Nonverbal aspects of communication are just as important, if not more important, than the verbal aspects.

- It is important to be aware of your own preferences for communicating.

- Early childhood professionals can help families foster their children's development when they are aware of the communication environment in which the children live.

- The interpreter and the provider must work together as a team.

- The role of the interpreter is to enhance communication, not to take the place of the service provider.

- An ideal interpreter has participated in formal training, is proficient in the languages of both parties, and is experienced in cross-cultural communication.

Reflecting and Getting Ready for Change

Before going on to the next module, reflect on these questions and carry out the suggestions that follow:

1. Do I like it when people look you in the eye when speaking with me?

2. When I am in a conversation with someone, how much physical space do I need between me and the other person? How much space do I need if the person is a friend or family member versus someone I just met?

3. How do I react to people who are learning English or have "accents" that are different from my own?

4. Is my usual communication style direct?

5. Do I talk more than I listen? How long do I wait for the other person to answer or respond to a question?

6. What messages do I communicate with my facial expression, posture, or tone of voice?

7. Practice active listening techniques.

8. Work with a colleague to increase comfort in communicating cross-culturally.

9. Try role playing, simulation, or videotaping to increase awareness and skills.

References

American Speech-Language-Hearing Association. (n.d.). *Accent modification.* Retrieved November 5, 2009, from http://www.asha.org/public/speech/development/accent_mod.htm

Angelelli, C. (2004). *Medical interpreting and cross-cultural communication.* Cambridge, United Kingdom: Cambridge University Press.

Berk, L.E. (2002). *Infants and children: Prenatal through middle childhood* (4th ed.). Boston: Allyn & Bacon.

Bowen, C. (1998). *Ages and stages: Developmental milestones for receptive and expressive language acquisition.* Retrieved September 28, 2008, from http://www.speech-language-therapy.com/devel2.htm

Chen, D., Chan, S., & Brekken, L. (Producers). (2000). *Conversations for three: Communicating through interpreters* [Videotape and booklet]. Baltimore: Paul H. Brookes Publishing Co.

Connecticut Birth to Three. (n.d.). *Safety tips.* Retrieved March 4, 2010, from http://www.birth23.org/Families/SafetyTips.asp

Cross-Cultural Health Care Program. (n.d.). *Mission.* Retrieved November 5, 2009, from http://www.xculture.org

D'Andrea, V.J., & Salovey, P. (Eds.). (1996). *Peer counseling: Skills, ethics and perspective* (2nd ed.). Palo Alto, CA: Science and Behavior Books.

Diversity Rx. (n.d.). *Overview of models and strategies for overcoming linguistic and cultural barriers to health care.* Retrieved November 5, 2009, from http://www.diversityrx.org/htm/MODELS.htm

Gray, J. (1992). *Men are from Mars, women are from Venus: A practical guide for improving communication and getting what you want in your relationships.* New York: HarperCollins.

Gudykunst, W.B. (2003). *Cross-cultural and intercultural communication.* Thousand Oaks, CA: Sage Publications.

Hall, E.T. (1981a). *Beyond culture.* New York: Doubleday.

Hall, E.T. (1981b). *The silent language.* New York: Doubleday.

Lynch, E.W., & Hanson, M.J. (Eds.). (2004). *Developing cross-cultural competence: A guide for working with children and their families* (3rd ed.). Baltimore: Paul H. Brookes Publishing Co.

Moore, S., Perez-Mendez, C., Beatty, J., & Eiserman, W. (1999). *A three-way conversation: Effective use of cultural mediators, interpreters and translators.* Denver, CO: Western Media Products.

National Center for Cultural Competence. (n.d.). *The research and evidence.* Retrieved November 5, 2009, from http://www11.georgetown.edu/research/gucchd/NCCC/research/index.html

National Center for Cultural Competence. (2004). *Bridging the cultural divide in health care settings: The essential role of cultural broker programs.* Washington, DC: Georgetown University Center for Child and Human Development, University Center for Excellence in Development Disabilities.

Ogulnick, K. (Ed.). (2000). *Language crossings: Negotiating the self in a multicultural world.* New York: Teacher's College Press.

Pinker, S. (1994). *The language instinct: How the mind creates language.* New York: HarperCollins.

Reed, V.A. (2005). *An introduction to children with language disorders* (3rd ed.). Upper Saddle River, NJ: Pearson Education.

Schwab, J., Baldwin, M., Gerber, J., Gomori, M., & Satir, V. (1989). *The Satir approach to communication: A workshop manual.* Palo Alto, CA: Science and Behavior Books.

Shin, H., with Bruno, R. (2003, October). Language use and English-speaking ability: 2000. *Census 2000 Brief.* Retrieved from http://www.census.gov/prod/2003pubs/c2kbr-29.pdf

Recommended Resources

Barrera, I., Corso, R.M., & Macpherson, D. (2003). S*killed dialogue: Strategies for responding to cultural diversity in early childhood.* Baltimore: Paul H. Brookes Publishing Co.

This book provides a model for understanding culture and diversity. It also provides strategies for learning and applying the essentials of Skilled Dialogue.

Bennett, M. J. (1998). *Basic concepts of intercultural communication.* Yarmouth, ME: Intercultural Press.

This is a collection of articles on intercultural communication written by preeminent scholars and practitioners in the field. The resource provides an introduction to intercultural communication and explores the complexities of intercultural relations more deeply for seasoned practitioners.

Catlett, C., Winton, P., & Hamel, S. (Eds.). (2004). *Resource guide: Selected early childhood/early intervention training materials* (12th ed.). Chapel Hill: The University of North Carolina at Chapel Hill, FPG Child Development Institute.

This guide provides descriptions of good, readily available, and low-cost instructional resources. It includes curricula, videotapes, discussion guides, books, and other resources for teaching, training, staff development, and supervision. The latest edition may be downloaded free-of-charge at http://www.fpg.unc.edu/~scpp/pdfs/rguide.pdf; it includes close to 600 entries, divided into 16 sections that correspond with key early childhood/early intervention topical areas.

Chen, D., Chan, S., & Brekken, L. (Producers). (2000). *Conversations for three: Communicating through interpreters* [Videotape and booklet]. Baltimore: Paul H. Brookes Publishing Co.

This videotape shows service providers how to respond sensitively to cultural and linguistic differences in order to promote effective communication when working with families and interpreters.

Langdon, H. (2003). *Working with interpreters to serve bilingual children and families* [Videotape and booklet] (ASHA Self-Study 6820). Rockville, MD: American Speech-Language-Hearing Association.

This videotape and its accompanying manual are designed to support professionals in learning about the importance of speech-language pathologists working effectively with interpreters, an approach to looking for an interpreter with the appropriate knowledge and skills, and the roles and responsibilities of the speech-language pathologist and interpreter in parent conference and client assessment.

Langdon, H.W., & Cheng, L-R.L. (2002). *Collaborating with interpreters and translators: A guide for communication disorders professionals*. Eau Claire, WI: Thinking Publications.

The authors discuss the roles, responsibilities, and ethical duties of interpreters, translators, speech-language pathologists, and audiologists. Information is provided about the characteristics of English language learners, including code switching, language loss, grammar, semantics, and other considerations for interpreters and translators.

Moore, S., Perez-Mendez, C., Beatty, J., & Eiserman, W. (1999). *A three-way conversation: Effective use of cultural mediators, interpreters and translators* [Videotape]. Denver, CO: Western Media Products.

This videotape explores key considerations by listening to families' and professionals' descriptions of effective uses of cultural mediators, interpreters, and translators in a variety of educational and intervention settings.

Ogulnick, K. (Ed.). (2000). *Language crossings: Negotiating the self in a multicultural world*. New York: Teachers College Press.

This is a collection of essays that explore the connections among language use, language learning, and cultural identity. These personal narratives represent a diversity of cultures, ages, and nationalities and illustrate the struggles and rewards of language learning as well as show the interconnectedness of language and identity.

Sharpe, P. (1994). *Beginning Spanish for teachers of Hispanic students*. Hauppauge, NY: Barron's Educational Series.

These materials help teachers learn to give instructions and communicate in Spanish with students who may be having trouble understanding English. The package includes four 90-minute cassettes, a read-along audioscript for the lessons, 370 dialogue cards with illustrations, and a book containing self-teaching study units.

Shirts, R.G. (1974). *Bafa'Bafa': A cross-cultural simulation*. Del Mar, CA: Simulation Training Systems.

This simulation is designed to make participants personally aware of the issues around culture differences. After an initial briefing, two cultures are created. The Alpha culture is a relationship-oriented, high-context, strong in-group–out-group culture. The Beta culture is a highly competitive trading culture. After the participants learn the rules of their culture and begin living it, observers and visitors are exchanged. This is followed by a debriefing, in which participants discuss the stereotyping, misperceptions, and misunderstandings that resulted from the shared experience.

Storti, C. (1994). *Cross-cultural dialogues: 74 brief encounters with cultural difference*. Yarmouth, ME: Intercultural Press.

According to the author, cultural misunderstandings in everyday conversation can cause confusion, irritation, and even alienation. These misunderstandings also undermine communication, threaten important relationships, and cost a great deal of time and money. This book is a collection of brief conversations between an American and someone from another country and culture. Each dialogue contains at least one breach of cultural norms, and the reader is challenged to figure it out. Ten cultures are represented in the dialogues: Arab/Middle Eastern, British, Chinese, French, German, Latino, Indian, Japanese, Mediterranean/European, and Russian.

Thiagarajan, S., & Stienwachs, B. (1990). *Barnga: A simulation game on cultural clashes.* Yarmouth, ME: Intercultural Press.

This card game is designed to help participants experience culture shock. People from different cultures have different ways of doing things that are sometimes very subtle. Barnga engages participants in a fun activity that will facilitate discovery and discussion about reconciling difference and functioning in a cross-cultural group.

Understanding Diverse Families and Their Roles

NEW VOICES
N V
NUEVAS VOCES

To understand child-rearing perspectives, values, and practices of families from diverse cultural and linguistic backgrounds, with an emphasis on those of Latino families

Objectives

- Understand child-rearing practices in diverse families

- Learn about Latino families' values, beliefs, and child-rearing practices

- Understand Latino families' perspectives on disabilities

- Learn strategies for building partnerships with Latino families

How children are raised within the context of their family's cultural values and beliefs has an influence on how children perceive, learn, and develop in their world. When early childhood professionals form strong partnerships with families and embrace the families' home culture, children flourish. This module discusses the importance of forming these partnerships and the strategies for welcoming and promoting the involvement of parents from culturally and linguistically diverse backgrounds in the care and education of their young children.

Specifically, this module discusses universal goals of child rearing that can be found across cultures and the different ways in which these goals are pursued depending on families' beliefs, needs, and priorities. The discussion of cross-cultural issues in child rearing is followed by child-rearing beliefs and values found among Latino families, their perspectives on children's disabilities, and strategies for promoting the involvement of Latino parents in early childhood programs.

Child Rearing Across Cultures

People from different parts of the world with different histories hold diverse beliefs about the nature and nurturing of children. Different cultures do not raise their children in the same way. Values, beliefs, customs, traditions, and past experiences all play a part in how parents raise their children (Harwood, Miller, & Irizarry, 1995). Therefore, parents' goals and expectations for their children's development are influenced by their culture. Likewise, the practitioners' views and expectations about children's development are influenced by their own cultural background.

Child-rearing practices in cultures different from our own may seem peculiar and sometimes unnatural, but they make sense when understood within the context of the particular society in which they originated (Keller, 2003; Rogoff, 2003). Child-rearing practices may reflect not only values and beliefs but also needs and availability of resources (e.g., the family's socioeconomic status) (Ogbu, 1994). Differences and similarities among parents' child-rearing goals and practices can be found across cultures and among members of the same cultural group regarding socioeconomic status. Differences in child-rearing practices and priorities may also be influenced by geographic location (e.g., living in rural versus urban or suburban settings). For example, in some cultures it is not uncommon for families to share a dwelling with extended family members; therefore, children in those families may have multiple caregivers. Raising the children becomes a family affair. Similarly, sharing clothing with siblings or cousins may be a necessity for some children; for children with membership in other groups, this may be a practice based on a cultural belief, regardless of the family's socioeconomic status. In the same way, several people using the same utensil and eating from the same plate may be common practice in some cultures yet may seem unhealthy in others.

Immigrant families, in particular, may face challenges raising their children in an environment that does not necessarily embrace the same values they have, those that were instilled in them by their own families. It is especially difficult when there are conflicting values between what children are taught in an early childhood program and what is being taught at home. In those situations, children are placed in the position of opting or choosing between supposedly "right" and "wrong" perspectives, with the family perspective usually being the "wrong" one. These incongruities may negatively affect the relationship between children and their families. The "Practicing Multicultural Early Care and Education" section in Module 5 discusses more extensively the impact of cultural incongruities between home and early childhood education settings.

Common Goals Across Cultures

Regardless of families' cultural background or experiences, there are some universal goals that all parents want to reach for their children:

- Providing for their children's physical, health, and safety needs

- Passing on the basic values and norms of their family and culture so their children can use these for guidance in making the appropriate decisions in life

- Helping their children become competent, contributing, and successful adults

There might be differences among families about their priorities and expectations for their children, and they may have different ideas about how they are going to achieve these goals for their children, but the bottom line is the same: provide for their children's well-being and successful future. With this in mind, as early childhood professionals we should make every effort to get to know the families of the children we are working with and develop an understanding of their perspectives.

As mentioned in Module 1, in order to be able to understand others' perspectives, we first need to learn about ourselves. Reflecting on our own experiences and the way we were raised helps us better understand others' child-rearing practices. Having in mind the goals mentioned above, here are some questions to help in this reflection:

- Are these goals similar to those that your parents had for you?

- Are these goals that you want for your own children?

- Are there other goals that transcend all cultures?

There might be different ways to achieve these goals and different priorities among families, but we all want the very best for our children.

Perspectives on Child Rearing

This section describes two distinct perspectives about children's development and learning that influence parents' child-rearing practices: individualism and collectivism (Greenfield et al., 2006). These perspectives can help in understanding diverse parents' priorities and expectations with regard to their children's development and education. These are idealized contrasting perspectives that do not represent an individual parent or family. Actually, it will be difficult to find a person that fits only one of these perspectives; parents usually incorporate elements of both perspectives when raising their children, giving emphasis to one of them.

Individualism

Some cultures tend to place emphasis on the individual. So, it is in child rearing that independence, personal choices, and self-expression become the focus of children's development and education (Greenfield, Keller, Fuligni, & Maynard, 2003).

From this perspective, families focus on teaching their children to be independent from an early age and teach them self-help skills, such as feeding themselves, using the toilet, and sleeping in one's own bed. Parents prefer not to hold babies for long periods of time but, rather, to put them on the floor and help them to explore by themselves, to crawl, and eventually to walk. Parents prefer to give children opportunities to make choices rather than making all of the decisions. Also, parents teach their children the importance of verbal communication. Regarding social relations, they place more emphasis on standing out and working independently; sharing is by choice (Greenfield et al., 2006).

In an early childhood program, the emphasis on individualism might be reflected in practices that focus on teaching children to learn how to work independently, putting more importance on individual activities and competitive games instead of activities that require children to work cooperatively. These programs might emphasize progress on cognitive and academic skills and pay less attention to the development of social skills. Also, in these programs children are expected to learn by asking questions and expressing curiosity. Think about your own values as a teacher or service provider:

- Can you see ways in which you emphasize individualism?

- Can you see ways in which your school or program emphasizes individualism?

Collectivism

In some cultures, the emphasis is not on the individual but, rather, on the collective whole. That means that children are expected and raised to be interdependent, to respect and revere their elders, to accept their gender and family roles, and to see themselves in the context of the whole group (Greenfield et al., 2003).

Families who emphasize collectivism in child rearing will be more concerned about teaching their children how to be a good member of the family, be supportive of their siblings, help out in family chores, and participate in family events than families sharing the individualism perspective. Other examples of child-rearing practices within the collectivism perspective include toddlers and preschoolers being fed by their mother or another family member, being held even though they know how to walk, and always or typically going with their parents to most family and community events.

Within the collectivism perspective, children are expected to learn through observing and paying close attention to what the adult is doing (Rogoff, 2003; Romero, 1994). When a teacher or service provider is focused on individualism (e.g., teaching a child to work independently), it may create a conflict and misinterpretation of the capabilities of children who have been socialized in a family whose emphasis is on social skills, respect, and cooperation. Furthermore, a teacher whose expectations are based on the belief that independence and a logical-scientific way of thinking are indicators of development and ability may misinterpret or dismiss some children's behaviors as incorrect or inappropriate. Martita's story illustrates this situation:

Ms. Brown asked children in her classroom to describe an apple. Martita raised her hand and started telling the teacher, "The other day, I was in the kitchen with my mom because she asked me to help her make a pie. . . ." Ms. Brown interrupted Martita and said, "I asked what an apple is." Then another student raised his hand and Ms. Brown said, "Okay, Jimmy, tell me what an apple is." Jimmy responded, "An apple is a fruit, is round, is red on the outside, and is yellowish in the inside." Ms. Brown said, "That is correct. Good job, Jimmy." Martita kept quiet for the rest of the school day.

Martita began by describing the social context in which she learned about the apple (i.e., helping her mom) before getting into the description, but her teacher thought that she had not understood the question. The consequence of the teacher dismissing Martita's answer was a situation in which Martita perceived herself and was perceived by her peers as not being competent for the task. Experiences such as the one illustrated here can have long-lasting negative effects on young children's academic performance and socioemotional development. What could this teacher have done differently to support this child's learning? Have you confronted a similar situation in your practice? (See Module 5 for strategies to help professionals address issues of conflicting perspectives between home and the early childhood setting).

It is important to keep in mind that, as mentioned in previous sections, many factors in addition to cultural background affect families' child-rearing practices, such as parents' level of education and socioeconomic status, residence in an urban or rural area, and acculturation level (for immigrant families), among others. It is very unlikely that you will encounter a family that represents exclusively one of these two child-rearing perspectives. Although families emphasize one of the two perspectives, most will incorporate practices that reflect both of these perspectives to some extent. As a general rule, do not make assumptions! Finding out about the beliefs and practices of the families of the children you are working with should be one of your priorities. Use that information when you are planning early childhood education or intervention services.

In the story below, Lake (1990) illustrated the differences between the development and learning priorities and expectations of a Native American father and his son's teacher. This father's child-rearing emphasized knowledge, values, and learning styles that were not part of what the teacher and the school expected for his son to be successful.

An Indian Father's Plea
Robert Lake (Medicine Grizzlybear)

I would like to introduce you to my son, Wind-Wolf. He is probably what you would consider a typical Indian kid. He was born and raised on a reservation. He has black hair, dark brown eyes, olive complexion. And like so many Indian children his age, he is shy and quiet in the classroom. He is 5 years old, in kindergarten, and I can't understand why you have already labeled him a "slow learner."

At the age of 5, he has already been through quite an education compared with his peers in Western society. At his first introduction into this world, he was bonded to his mother and to the Mother Earth in a traditional native childbirth ceremony. And he has been continuously cared for by his mother, father, sisters, cousins, uncles, grandparents, and extended tribal family since this ceremony.

From his mother's warm and loving arms, Wind-Wolf was placed in a secure and specially designed Indian baby basket. His father and the medicine elders conducted another ceremony with him that served to bond him with the essence of his genetic father, the Great Spirit, the Grandfather Sun, and the Grandmother Moon. This was all done in order to introduce him properly into the new and natural world, not the world of artificiality, and to protect his sensitive and delicate soul. It is our people's way of showing the newborn respect, ensuring that he starts his life on the path of spirituality.

The traditional Indian baby basket became his "turtle's shell" and served as the first seat for his classroom. He was strapped in for safety, protected from injury by the willow roots and hazel wood construction. The basket was made by a tribal elder who had gathered her materials with prayer and in a ceremonial way. It is the same kind of basket that our people have used for thousands of years. It is specially designed to provide the child with the kind of knowledge and experience he will need in order to survive in his culture and environment.

Wind-Wolf was strapped in snuggly with a deliberate restriction upon his arms and legs. Although you in Western society may argue that such a method serves to hinder motor-skill development and abstract reasoning, we believe it forces the child to first develop his intuitive faculties, rational intellect, symbolic thinking, and five senses. Wind-Wolf was with his mother constantly, closely bonded physically, as she carried him on her back or held him in front while breast-feeding. She carried him everywhere she went, and every night he slept with both parents. Because of this, Wind-Wolf's educational setting was not only a "secure" environment, but it was also very colorful, complicated, sensitive, and diverse. He has been with his mother at the ocean at daybreak when she made her prayers and gathered fresh seaweed from the rocks, he has sat with his uncles in a rowboat on the river while they fished with gill nets, and he has watched and listened to elders as they told creation stories and animal legends and sang songs around the campfires.

He has attended the sacred and ancient White Deerskin Dance of his people and is well-acquainted with the cultures and languages of other tribes. He has been with his mother when she gathered herbs for healing and watched his tribal aunts and grandmothers gather and prepare traditional foods such as acorn, smoked salmon, eel, and deer meat. He has played with abalone shells, pine nuts, iris grass string, and leather while watching the women make beaded jewelry and traditional native regalia. He has had many opportunities to watch his father, uncles, and ceremonial leaders using different kinds of songs while preparing for the sacred dances and rituals.

As he grew older, Wind-Wolf began to crawl out of the baby basket, develop his motor skills, and explore the world around him. When frightened or sleepy, he could always return to the basket as a turtle withdraws into its shell. Such an inward journey allows one to reflect in privacy on what he has learned and to carry the new knowledge deeply into the unconscious and the soul. Shapes, sizes, colors, texture, sound, smell feeling, taste, and the learning process are therefore functionally integrated—the physical and spiritual, matter and energy, conscious and unconscious, individual and social.

This kind of learning goes beyond the basics of distinguishing the difference between rough and smooth, hard and soft, black and white, similarities and extremes. For example, Wind-Wolf was with his mother in South Dakota while she danced for seven days straight in the hot sun, fasting, and piercing herself in the sacred Sun Dance Ceremony of a distant tribe. He has been doctored in a number of different healing ceremonies by medicine men and women from diverse places ranging from Alaska and Arizona to New York and California. He has been in more than 20 different sacred sweat-lodge rituals—used by native tribes to purify the mind, body, and soul—since he was 3 years old, and he has already been exposed to many different religions of his racial brothers: Protestant, Catholic, Asian Buddhist, and Tibetan Lamaist.

It takes a long time to absorb and reflect on these kinds of experiences, so maybe that is why you think my Indian child is a slow learner. His aunts and grandmothers taught him to count and know his numbers while they sorted out the complex materials used to make the abstract designs in the native baskets. He listened to his mother count each and every bead and sort out numerically according to color while she painstakingly made complex beaded belts and necklaces. He learned his basic numbers by helping his father count and sort the rocks to be used in the sweat-lodge—seven rocks for a medicine sweat, say, or 13 for the summer solstice ceremony. (The rocks are later heated and doused with water to create purifying steam.) And he was taught to learn mathematics by counting the sticks we use in our traditional native hand game. So I realize he may be slow in grasping the methods and tools that you are now using in you classroom, ones quite familiar to his white peers, but I hope you will be patient with him. It takes time to adjust to a new cultural system and learn new things.

He is not culturally "disadvantaged," but he is culturally "different." If you ask him how many months there are in a year, he will probably tell you 13. He will respond this way not because he doesn't know how to count properly, but because he has been taught by our traditional people that there are 13 full moons in a year according to the native tribal calendar and that there are really 13 planets in our solar system and 13 tail feathers on a perfectly balanced eagle, the most powerful kind of bird to use in ceremonial healing.

But he also knows that some eagles may only have 12 tail feathers, or seven, that they do not all have the same number. He knows that the flicker has exactly 10 tail feathers; that they are red and black, representing the directions of east and west, life and death; and that this bird is considered a "fire" bird, a power used in native doctoring and healing. He can probably count more than 40 different kinds of birds, tell you and his peers what kind of bird each is and where it lives, the seasons in which it appears, and how it is used in a sacred ceremony. He may also have trouble writing his name on a piece of paper, but he knows how to say it and many other things in several different Indian languages. He is not fluent yet because he is only 5 years old and required by law to attend your educational system, learn your language, your values, your ways of thinking, and your methods of teaching and learning.

So you see, all of these influences together make him somewhat shy and quiet—and perhaps "slow" according to your standards. But if Wind-Wolf was not prepared for his first tentative foray into your world, neither were you appreciative of his culture. On the first day of class, you had difficulty with his name. You wanted to call him Wind, insisting that Wolf must somehow be his middle name. The students in the class laughed at him, causing further embarrassment.

While you were trying to teach him your new methods, helping him learn new tools for self-discovery and adapt to his new learning environment, he may be looking out the window as if daydreaming. Why? Because he has been taught to watch and study the changes in nature. It is hard for him to make the appropriate psychic switch from the right to the left hemisphere of the brain when he sees the leaves turning bright colors, the geese heading south, and the squirrels scurrying around for nuts to get ready for a harsh winter. In his heart, in his young mind, and almost by instinct, he knows that this is the time of the year he is supposed to be with people gathering and preparing fish, deer meat, and native plants and herbs, and learning his assigned tasks in this role. He is caught between two worlds, torn by two distinct cultural systems.

Yesterday, for the third time in two weeks, he came home crying and said he wanted to have his hair cut. He said he doesn't have any friends at school because they make fun of his long hair. I tried to explain to him that in our culture, long hair is a sign of masculinity and balance and is a source of power. But he remained adamant in his position.

To make matters worse, he recently encountered his first harsh case of racism. Wind-Wolf had managed to adopt at least one good school friend. On the way home from school one day, he asked his new pal if he wanted to come home to play with him until supper. That was OK with Wind-Wolf's mother, who was walking with them. When they all got to the little friend's house, the two boys ran inside to ask permission while Wind-Wolf's mother waited. But the other boy's mother lashed out: "It is OK if you have to play with him at school, but we don't allow those kind of people in our house!" When my wife asked why not, the other boy's mother answered, "Because you are Indians, and we are white, and I don't want my kids growing up with your kind of people."

So now my young Indian child does not want to go to school anymore (even though we cut his hair). He feels that he does not belong. He is the only Indian child in your class, and he is well-aware of this fact. Instead of being proud of his race, heritage, and culture, he feels ashamed. When he watches television, he asks why the white people hate us so much and always kill our people in the movies and why they take everything away from us. He asks why the other kids in school are not taught about the power, beauty, and essence of nature or provided with an opportunity to experience the world around them firsthand. He says he hates living in the city and that he misses his Indian cousins and friends. He asks why one young white girl at school who is his friend always tells him, "I like you, Wind-Wolf, because you are a good Indian."

Now he refuses to sing his native songs, play with his Indian artifacts, learn his language, or participate in his sacred ceremonies. When I ask him to go to an urban powwow or help me with a sacred sweat-lodge ritual, he says no because "that's weird" and he doesn't want his friends at school to think he doesn't believe in God.

So, dear teacher, I want to introduce you to my son, Wind-Wolf, who is not really a "typical" little Indian kid after all. He stems from a long line of hereditary chiefs, medicine men and women, and ceremonial leaders whose accomplishments and unique forms of knowledge are still being studied and recorded in contemporary books. He has seven different tribal systems flowing through his blood; he is even part white. I want my child to succeed in school and in life. I don't want him to be a dropout or juvenile delinquent or to end up on drugs and alcohol because he is made to feel inferior or because of discrimination. I want him to be proud of his rich heritage and culture, and I would like him to develop the necessary capabilities to adapt to, and succeed in, both cultures. But I need your help.

What you say and what you do in the classroom, what you teach and how you teach it, and what you don't say and don't teach will have a significant effect on the potential success or failure of my child. Please remember that this is the primary year of his education and development. All I ask is that you work with me, not against me, to help educate my child in the best way. If you don't have the knowledge, preparation, experience, or training to effectively deal with culturally different children, I am willing to help you with the few resources I have available or direct you to such resources.

Millions of dollars have been appropriated by Congress and are being spent each year for "Indian Education." All you have to do is take advantage of it and encourage your school to make an effort to use it in the name of "equal education." My Indian child has a constitutional right to learn, retain, and maintain his heritage and culture. By the same token, I strongly believe that non-Indian children also have a constitutional right to learn about our Native American heritage and culture, because Indians play a significant part in the history of Western society. Until this reality is equally understood and applied in education as a whole, there will be a lot more schoolchildren in grades K-2 identified as "slow learners."

My son, Wind-Wolf, is not an empty glass coming into your class to be filled. He is a full basket coming into a different environment and society with something special to share. Please let him share his knowledge, heritage, and culture with you and his peers.

[Lake reports that Wind-Wolf, now 8, is doing better in school, but the boy's struggle for cultural identity continues.]

Robert Lake (Medicine Grizzlybear) is a member of the Seneca and Cherokee Indian tribes, and is an associate professor of education at Gonzaga University.

From Lake, R. (Medicine Grizzlybear). (1990). An Indian father's plea. *Teacher Magazine, 2*(1), 48–53; reprinted by permission.

Latino Cultural Perspectives and Child Rearing

Yo creo que respeto . . . ¡la educación! yo creo que eso es lo más, más importante para mí, que estén educados, que sean respetuosos. Y enseñarles también a tener todas nuestras tradiciones. Ahí vienen los valores, ¿no? Entonces para mi es muy importante, no porque esté aquí [en los Estados Unidos] perder todo lo que yo traigo de mi cultura, de mi país. Entonces yo siempre les estoy inculcando a mis hijos las tradiciones, los valores que nosotros traemos y que no se pierdan. Nosotros hacemos por ahí . . . oh! Las Posadas. Hacemos Posadas o a veces les recuerdo "Hoy es el 16 de septiembre, una fecha muy importante para México", y [mi hijo] me pregunta: "¿Qué pasó?" y entonces yo les empiezo a platicar lo que pasó ese día en México, y . . . oh! en el Día de los Muertos, ¿porqué se hace esto?" y como nos ve hacerlo . . . hacemos un altar entonces el empieza a preguntar y yo ya le empiezo a platicar "en México se hace esto, se hace pan, se pone comida". Entonces yo trato de transmitirle, no solo con palabras sino también con hechos, para que el niño vaya absorbiendo nuestras tradiciones y nuestros valores porque de ahí sale todo.

I believe that respect . . . educación* is most important, that my children are well educated and well behaved, that they are respectful people. And they should be taught our traditions. It's from there that all the values come from, right? That is very important for me. Just because I am now living here [in the United States] doesn't mean I should lose everything I bring with me from my culture, my country. That is why I am always teaching my children our traditions and values, so that they are not lost. We celebrate for instance . . . oh! Las Posadas. We do Posadas, or sometimes I remind them "Today is September 16th, a very important day in Mexico," and [my son] asks: "What happened?" then, I start telling them what happened that day in Mexico. Oh! And on the Day of the Dead, why is this done? And since he sees us doing it . . . we make an altar, then he starts asking and I start telling him, "In Mexico we do this, we make bread, we bring food." So, I try to transmit [communicate] to him not only with words but by doing things, so that the child starts assimilating our traditions and values, because that is from which everything else comes from.

—*Margarita, Mexico*

The importance of involving the family in the education of young children and offering early intervention services that are family centered are core principles of the early childhood care and education field. The implementation of practices that follow these principles requires early childhood professionals to acknowledge the diversity of beliefs and values about child rearing that may exist among families in their programs, so that practices promoting or increasing family involvement are effective in reaching out to all families.

(*Certain words cannot be translated because the word that can be used for the translation does not have the exact same meaning.)

This section presents information that can help professionals better understand the child-rearing perspectives of Latino families. After reviewing the research literature, we chose to include here child-rearing perspectives that are common among Latino families from different national origins, socioeconomic status levels, and lengths of residency in the United States. However, it must be emphasized that the intent is to provide information that can be used as a starting point when approaching Latino families. You are strongly encouraged not to make assumptions about Latino families (or any family!). Instead, as part of your program planning, you should incorporate activities aimed at finding out about the families you are working with in your programs.

Child-Rearing Values Among Latino Families

Familism, *respeto*, and *educación* are important concepts to most Latino families. Each of theses values is discussed next.

La Familia: Familism as a Prevalent Characteristic

Yo tengo muchos hermanos aquí y [mis] hijos conviven mucho con sus hijos [primos], y sus hijos con los míos. Entonces cuando vienen a casa es como una parte que me toca a mí, como estar pendiente de ellos, que si me dicen, "Tía, ¿me puedo comer esto?" Yo les digo, "No, porque todavía no has comido," o "Tía, ¿me dejas salir afuera?" "No, porque hace mucho calor," o "Más tarde," o algo así. Entonces yo creo que [los tíos] participan mucho en la educación de mis hijos porque hay mucha comunicación y siempre están yendo para allá con ellos y ellos los reprenden a veces en algo, influyen en la educación. Si hizo algo malo, por ejemplo, si está peleando con el primo lo reprenden. Le dicen, "Carlos, no debes hacer esto, no debes pelear." Yo a veces que vienen [mis sobrinos] y están todos peleando y están viendo la televisión, yo apago la televisión, "No van a ver la TV porque se pelearon o porque discutieron."

I have many siblings here, and the children spend a lot of time with their children [cousins]. When they come over it is my responsibility to be attentive to them. If they say to me, "Aunt, can I eat this [dessert]?" I tell them, "No, because you still haven't eaten [dinner]," or, "Aunt, can I go outside?" "No, because it is very hot," or, "Later," or something like that. So I believe that [aunts and uncles] participate a lot in the education of my children because there is a lot of communication and they are always going over there with them, and sometimes they reprimand them about something, they influence my children's education. If he did something bad, for example, if he is fighting with his cousin, they reprimand him. They tell him, "Carlos, you shouldn't do this; you shouldn't fight." Sometimes they [my nephews] come and sometimes they are all fighting and they are watching television, I turn off the television. "You aren't going to watch TV because you were fighting or arguing."

—*Lupe, Mexico*

Familism is a strong identification with and attachment to the family, marked by strong feelings of loyalty, reciprocity, and solidarity among family members (Vega, 1995). It includes the extended network of blood relatives, compadres (godparents), and in-laws. It is not uncommon to find Latinos living in trigenerational households. Depending on their length of residency in the United States, members of Latino households may also include unmarried siblings or cousins of the husband or wife (Hurtado, 1995). Extended family networks provide a sense of cultural identity and social support. The family provides help both financially and emotionally. Latinos desire to be geographically close to their family members (Bender & Castro, 2000; Sabogal, Marín, Otero-Sabogal, Marín, & Perez-Stable, 1987); this characteristic is prevalent among Latinos of different national origins, socioeconomic status levels, and acculturation levels (Keefe & Padilla, 1987; Zambrana, 1995). There are three components of familism:

1. *Family obligations:* Family members are expected to assist each other by offering material and emotional support, particularly in times of hardship. There is a sense of responsibility for the well-being of the entire family.

2. *Family help:* Family members rely on other family members for support. This is illustrated by the expression, "En nadie puedes confiar tanto como en tu familia" ["You cannot trust anybody else more than you trust your family"]. When facing a problem, one would look for help first among family members. *La familia* is always there to offer unconditional support.

3. *Family guidance:* Important decisions are made with advice from significant family members (e.g., asking for opinions or advice from one's grandparents, parents, or spouse).

Respeto

El respeto . . . Yo siempre estoy hablando con él [mi hijo]. Bueno él es muy abierto ahorita con nosotros, nos habla de tú y yo a veces le comento que yo a mi papá y a mi mamá nunca les hablaba de tú, les hablaba de usted, y él dice, "Mami ¿entonces?", yo digo, "Bueno a mi me gusta que hables de tú, pero tú a mi no me puedes gritar, no me puedes tratar de pegar, no puedes. . . ." A veces le digo, "Cuando una persona mayor te esté corrigiendo, escúchala, y si tu ves que algo tu le puedes decir, pues bien, pero no te puedes molestar con una persona mayor o contestar. Primero tienes que escuchar lo que te esta diciendo." Y así yo le voy enseñando [a mi hijo] que debe tener respeto a las personas mayores. No sé, yo tengo mucho eso . . . como a mí me inculcaron mucho respeto a mis

Respect . . . I am always talking with my son [about respect]. He is very open with us right now, he addresses us using the informal "you," and I sometimes tell him that I never talked to my parents that way, it was always as "Usted" [more formal, respectful]. Then, he asks, "Mommy, then what should I do?" I say, "Well, I like that you address me as 'you' [informal], but you cannot yell at me, you cannot hit me, you cannot. . . ." Sometimes I tell him, "When someone older than you is corrigiéndote*, listen to that person, you may have something to say, too, and that is okay but you cannot get mad at that person or talk back to that person. First you have to listen to what that person is telling you." And that is how I go about teaching my child that he has to treat older persons with respect. I don't know,

papás [yo le digo], "Carlos a tu papá no le debes gritar, o con el tío no debes jugar". Él es muy juguetón con sus tíos . . . Y él me pregunta porque. "Porque no. Porque te ves mal. Porque tú eres niño y él es una persona mayor," y así trato de infundirle respeto a las personas mas que nada.

that is important for me, since I was inculcated to respect my parents. I say to my son, "Carlos, you should not behave like that," or "You should not play with your uncle like that." He is very playful with his uncles. He asks why. "Because you are a child and he is an adult," and that is how I try to teach him that above all, he has to respect people.

—*Lupe, Mexico*

(*Certain words cannot be translated because the word that can be used for the translation does not have the exact same meaning.)

Respeto is a set of behaviors that acknowledge an individual's position in the family, community, or institution (Valdés, 1996). It involves demonstrating personal regard, such as listening to one's grandparents' advice. Those deserving *respeto* include authority figures—for example one's parents, older siblings (seen as role models), and grandparents. *Faltar al respeto* (to offend someone's sense of dignity) is considered a serious affront. For example, talking back to one's parents is considered a *falta de respeto* (a lack of respect).

Teachers are usually considered very important authority figures. They are seen as the experts who know what is best for the education of children. In many cases, Latino parents will not question what a teacher recommends. Children are taught to show *respeto* for their teachers by following directions and never confronting or challenging what the teacher says.

Un Niño Bien Educado: The Concept of Educación

Yo quisiera estar con mi nena igual como pude estar con mi hijo, aunque en este país no se puede. La mamá lava, cocina, y hace todo, y está con los hijos, eso para mí es muy importante. Yo soy maestra; sé que en los primeros cuatro o cinco años de un niño es importante que esté con la mamá. Ella es la primera educadora del niño para que sus hijos sean en el futuro buenas personas, porque en la escuela no lo van a educar igual que la mamá. En la escuela te enseñan los números, las letras. Es más intelectual, y no lo que es más importante, lo espiritual, los valores.

I would like to be with my baby as much as I was able to be with my son, even though you can't in this country. The mother cleans, cooks, and does everything, and stays with the children, this is very important to me. I am a teacher; I know that it is important for a child to be with her mother during her first four or five years. She is the child's first educator so that her children are good people in the future, because at school they aren't going to educate a child like a mother does. At school they teach you numbers, letters. It is more intellectual, and not what is most important, the

(*Certain words cannot be translated because the word that can be used for the translation does not have the exact same meaning.)

Eso no te van a enseñar en la escuela. Entonces, por eso, yo trato de trabajar con ella, y se me hace difícil porque acá lo primero que te dicen es, "Ponle en una guardería." Yo he trabajado en guardería y he visto como los niños de tres semanas de nacidos ya van para allá, y eso es terrible; a mí eso me rompe el corazón. Yo he tratado y estoy tratando de no hacer eso con mi hija."

spiritual, the values. They aren't going to teach you that at school. Therefore, I try to work with her, and it is difficult for me because here the first thing people tell you is, "Put her in a child care." I have worked at a child care and I have seen how the children three weeks old already go there, and that is terrible, that breaks my heart. I have tried and am still trying not to do that with my daughter."

—*Elena, Puerto Rico*

The concept of *educación* refers to the total task of bringing up a moral and responsible child. It means teaching children important lessons, such as the difference between right and wrong, respect for parents and elders, and good manners. The concept of *educación* cannot be translated as *education,* as the latter strictly refers to the level of formal instruction that a person has received. In Latino culture, *educación* is a broader concept that includes formal instruction but also focuses on being a moral, well-behaved, and responsible person. A Latin American saying explains this idea clearly: "La educación empieza por casa" ["Being well-educated comes from home"].

Families use *consejos,* spontaneous teachable moments, to educate and teach their children. They use *dichos y refranes* (sayings and proverbs) to give their children lessons about life: how to be a good, well-behaved, well-mannered person; how to share; how to respect their elders; and so forth. In particular, Latino mothers believe that their role as "educators" of their children requires that they engage constantly in the practice of *dando consejos* (guiding their children), and they do it as often as possible and at no set schedule. For example, it can happen casually while performing household chores (Valdés, 1996).

> *Educación* is more than formal instruction or academic preparation.

Dichos y Refranes [Sayings and Proverbs]

This section lists *dichos y refranes* commonly used in different Latin American countries. Translations are included for all of them, and English equivalents are included when available. Do any of them sound familiar to you? Are similar sayings used in your own family and community?

Compassion and Reciprocity

- Amor con amor se paga.
  Translation: Love with love is paid (Aparicio, 1998, p. 57).
  English equivalent: One good turn deserves another (Aparicio, 1998, p. 57).

- El que parte y reparte se queda con la mejor parte.
  Translation: The person who divides and shares will have the better part.
  English equivalent: It's better to give than to receive.

Hard Work

- No dejes para mañana lo que puedas hacer hoy.
  Translation: Don't leave for tomorrow what you can do today.
  English equivalent: Never put off until tomorrow what you can do today (Aparicio, 1998, p. 87).

- El flojo trabaja doble.
  Translation: The lazy one works twice as hard.

- La ociosidad es madre de todos los vicios.
  Translation: Laziness is the mother of all vices.
  English equivalent: Idle hands are the Devil's workshop.

- Mas vale pájaro en mano que ciento volando.
  Translation: It is better to have a bird in hand than a hundred flying.
  English equivalent: A bird in the hand is worth two in the bush (Aparicio, 1998, p. 107).

Family Relationships

- La caridad empieza por casa.
  Translation and English equivalent: Charity begins at home.

- Candil de la calle, oscuridad de su casa.
  Translation: Light in the streets, darkness at home.

- En casa del herrero, cuchillo de palo.
  Translation: In the house of the blacksmith, wooden knives are used.
  English equivalent: The cobbler's children go barefoot.

Responsibility and Courage

- Cumple con tu deber, aunque tengas que perder.
  Translation: Carry out your duty, even if you have to lose.

- No hay mal que por bien no venga.
  Translation: There is no evil that does not bring some good.
  English equivalent: Every cloud has a silver lining (Aparicio, 1998, p. 67).

Educación

- Lo cortés no quita lo valiente.
  Translation: Being courteous does not mean you are not brave.

- Lo que se aprende en la cuna, hasta la sepultura.
  Translation: What you learn in the cradle lasts until you are in the tomb.

- No desprecies los consejos de los sabios, ni los viejos.
  Translation: Don't despise the advice from the wise or the elders.

- El árbol que crece torcido nunca su rama endereza.
  Translation: The tree that grows crooked can never be straightened.
  English equivalent: As the twig is bent, so grows the tree (Aparicio, 1998, p. 30).

Money

- Cuentas arregladas, amistades largas.
  Translation: Settled accounts, long friendship.
  English equivalent: Lend your money and lose your friend.

- Poderoso caballero es Don Dinero
  Translation: Mr. Money is a powerful gentleman.
  English equivalent: Money talks.

- La ambición rompe el saco.
  Translation: Ambition breaks the bag.

Health

- Desayuna como rico, almuerza como pobre y cena como mendigo.
  Translation: Eat breakfast like a wealthy person, eat lunch like a poor person, and eat dinner like a beggar.

- El que mucho abarca poco aprieta.
  Translation: He who spreads out too much squeezes little.
  English equivalent: Don't spread yourself too thin (Aparicio, 1998, p. 92).

- No por mucho madrugar, amanece más temprano.
  Translation: The sun will not rise sooner because you wake up earlier.

Relationships

- Al que a buen árbol se arrima, buena sombra le cobija.
  Translation: If you stay next to a good tree, a good shade will cover you.

- La manzana podrida corrompe a su compañera.
  Translation: A spoiled apple will spoil the ones next to it.
  English equivalent: One bad apple can spoil the bunch.

- Quien con lobos anda a aullar aprende.
  Translation: He who walks with wolves learns to howl.
  English equivalent: If you lie down with dogs, you will get up with fleas (Aparicio, 1998, p. 60).

Honesty

- Bienes mal adquiridos a nadie han enriquecido.
  Translation: Being dishonest will not make you rich.
  English equivalent: Cheaters never prosper.

- El que respeta lo ajeno està en paz.
  Translation: He who respects others' property lives in peace.

- Quien mal anda, mal acaba.
  Translation: He who lives a bad life will end badly.

Working with Latino Families of Children with Disabilities

Ana, 30 years old, was born in Mexico and arrived in the United States 4 years ago. She has a degree in business administration from a Mexican university. She is married and has a 2-year-old son, who was born with a cleft palate and without one ear. Here is her story translated from Spanish.

Ana's Story

When I went to my last ultrasound, my baby was sitting completely. In previous ultrasounds, my baby was always "eating" his finger, and the doctor would say to me, "Oh, your baby is very hungry; you don't feed him enough." In this last ultrasound she said to me, "Your baby will be born with a cleft palate." Until then, I didn't know that this was happening with my baby, and I felt very bad. The doctor only told me, "He is coming with that little defect, but he will have surgery and will be just fine, don't worry." I think she knew what was happening with my baby from previous ultrasounds, but she did not tell me. Maybe, I am not right. I don't know. When my child was born, I noticed that he also did not have one ear. The doctors told me that there was not an explanation about a cause, that it could be hereditary.

After delivering my baby at the hospital, I felt weak, even though I was fine during my pregnancy. The day after the delivery, the doctor wanted me to walk and get ready to go home, but I did not feel well. My husband talked with the doctor, but she said that I was doing very well. I delivered my baby on a Saturday and they wanted me to leave the hospital the following Monday. I felt so weak and tired. My husband insisted, fighting with the doctors until finally she agreed to perform an exam and found out that they had left a piece of placenta inside my body! Another doctor came after that and said to my husband, "Your wife is like a car; she only needs some gasoline and she'll be all right." My husband said, "My wife is not any car!" If my husband would have not been so firm with the doctors, I could have died.

One has to talk to them [the professionals] firmly and strongly; otherwise they do not pay attention to you. Many times, they have looked at me with scorn and talked to me loudly, in a bad mood. I defend myself with nothing but a strong look, saying, "No speak English." Thank God I went to the university in Mexico and understand some English. But sometimes when you feel emotionally fragile, you understand nothing, nothing of what is being said to you. And that is when you feel that shock, having someone talking to you loudly and you not being able to understand!

There were several issues that Ana's family had to contend with while she was in the hospital. First, Ana knew that her baby would have "a little defect" that would require surgery after he was born. She felt bad about this, but she also thought that her doctor knew earlier but did not tell her. Second, at birth, she saw that her baby was missing an ear. And third, even though Ana felt weak and sick after delivery, she was about to be discharged from the hospital. If her husband had not insisted that something was wrong, she believes that she would have died.

The parents, already emotionally fragile as they struggled with the realization of having a child with a disability, were not listened to, were talked to loudly, looked at scornfully, and had medical needs that were not taken care of. The fact that Ana, the mother, did not speak much English and no one tried to help her understand the situation is an example of the lack of cultural responsiveness by the hospital staff. The lack of sensitive and culturally responsive care increased the pain and stress that this family had to undergo and made them distrust the system.

If you were in the same situation, how would you respond? What if your doctor compared you to a car that needed gasoline? How would you feel living in a country where you did not know how the system worked or where to go for help? What if you were living here with a child with disabilities and you were not sure whether the doctors would pay attention to you? A little unsettling, isn't it?

How Do Latino Families Understand Disability?

Families from diverse cultural and ethnic backgrounds also hold diverse views on what can cause a disability and how to cope with it in the context of their families and communities. Latino families may link biomedical causes of disability to "spiritual phenomenon" or sociocultural beliefs. Therefore, they may welcome religious faith and folk practices into the process of healing, combining them with formal medical and therapeutic intervention services. Religious faith plays a critical role in the lives of many Latino families of children with disabilities, giving them spiritual and emotional support (Skinner, Correa, Skinner, & Bailey, 2001). For example, families may offer prayers or novenas, make mantas (promises) to religious figures, or make pilgrimages to holy sites. They may do this to ask for help with their child with a disability, for strength to cope with stress, and for the ability to give their child the support that he or she needs.

Depending on the family's beliefs and experiences, folk practices may be mixed with Christianity, such as using the services of *curanderos* (spiritual folk healers), who may use herbs, massages with ointments, and prayers. As an early childhood provider, it is important to show respect and learn about families' beliefs and understandings of disability. Listening to families will help you interpret what is behind their decisions and behaviors in relation to their child with disabilities. It may explain why a parent may be reluctant to follow certain recommendations or why he or she will not accept a particular kind of therapy.

Karen is a physical therapist who does not speak Spanish, but she knows how valuable cultural sensitivity is in dealing with families that have young children. She shared this experience:

I was filling in at an orthopedic clinic when a Latino mother and child came in for a physical therapy session. The child was wearing an amulet, which the physician asked her to remove to avoid danger of choking. The mother got upset and didn't want it removed. Through an interpreter, we were able to talk to the mother, and we found out that this was a protective necklace. We asked if she could pin it to her child's clothing, which she agreed to do.

If you ask questions and develop an understanding, you are more likely to be able to deal with dilemmas in a way that is acceptable to everyone.

Extended families are often the main source of support for Latino families with children with disabilities. Knowing that *la familia* plays a central role in the lives of Latino families, do not be surprised when extended family members are involved in making decisions related to the child's disability and care. The extended family provides support to, and needed respite care for, the parents. There may be Latino families who do not have relatives living close by, as might be the case for immigrant families; these families may feel isolated and thus be at higher risk for stress and depression because they lack the support of extended family.

There are differences among Latino families' perspectives on disabilities, depending on country of origin, education level, socioeconomic status, and acculturation, among other factors. There will always be variability among families' beliefs, and that is why the most important lesson to be learned is to keep ongoing communication with the family. Take the time to ask about all the things that you, as a professional, need to know in order to provide early intervention services that are culturally and linguistically appropriate.

Latino Families' Access to and Utilization of Early Childhood and Intervention Services

Latino families are at increased risk for lack of access to and underutilization of services (Arcia, Keyes, Gallagher, & Herrick, 1993; Ginsberg, 1992). They report greater need for information about how to get services, compared with parents in other racial or ethnic groups, and they have a greater level of need overall (Bailey, Skinner, Rodriguez, Gut, & Correra, 1999; Heller, Markwardt, Rowitz, & Farber, 1994; Sontag, Schacht, Horn, & Lenz, 1993). Many Latino families lack familiarity with U.S. education and health and human services systems and, more specifically, with the early intervention system. In addition, they may not be aware of how to seek help or gain access to these services appropriately. For example, in some Latin American countries, there is no an equivalent to an early intervention system to serve young children with developmental disabilities; therefore, Latino parents may not realize these services are available in the United States. There are other barriers as well. Some Latino parents may not feel at ease if their English language skills are limited; Spanish may or may not be their home language; in fact, they may speak an indigenous language. Lack of transportation, no access to child care for their other children, work demands, long hours, and schedules that do not mirror the typical 9-to-5 model contribute to the underutilization of services by Latino families.

The combination of rapid growth of the Latino population and the underutilization of services by Latino families has challenged health, education, and social service organizations across the country to follow the mandates of the Individuals with Disabilities Education Improvement Act of 2004 (IDEA 2004; PL 108-446) in relation to these families—that is, to support families in 1) learning about their child's disability, 2) becoming aware of their child's educational and therapeutic needs, 3) identifying the range of services that can potentially support them and their child, and 4) gaining access to those services. Some early intervention services have a distance to go before meeting these mandates. For example, Latino families of Mexican and Puerto Rican origin have reported a lower degree of satisfaction with services than non-Latino parents. Dissatisfaction with early intervention services is not always the result of the characteristics of the child (e.g., severity of disability, age) or the family (e.g., education level, English language proficiency) alone but is more likely to occur when program characteristics do not match the needs of the family, as in the case of Spanish-speaking families who reported not having access to materials in Spanish or to an interpreter or perceived service providers as being unwilling to help (Bailey et al., 1999).

Regarding access to early care and education for their young children, there are three critical issues affecting Latino families: 1) the low rate of utilizing licensed or registered child care, 2) the low percentage receiving subsidies, and 3) the quality of the child care that they do obtain. Latino families have the lowest child care utilization rates compared to all other racial and ethnic groups in the United States.

The National Center for Education Statistics (2006) reported that although 59% of Caucasian and 66% of African American children ages 3–5 attended some form of center-based child care program in 2005, only 43% of Latino children did so, with an even lower percentage (36%) among Latino children in poverty. Regarding subsidy use, among children living in poverty, the percentage of Latino children receiving subsidies is significantly lower than that of either African American or Caucasian children (5% versus 24% and 17%, respectively) (Kinukawa, Guzman, & Lippman, 2004).

Another critical issue is the quality of the child care used by Latino families. There is growing evidence that high-quality early care and education for 3- and 4-year-olds can have a positive impact on young children's later school success (Bowman, Donovan, & Burns, 2001; Magnuson & Waldfogel, 2005). However, the lower participation rate of Latino children in child care programs does not account entirely for the disparity that exists between Latino children and other groups with respect to readiness for kindergarten. Even among those who have attended an early childhood program, Latino children lag behind their peers when they enter kindergarten, and the gap in academic achievement appears to widen as children grow older. Nationally, Latino children have obtained the lowest mean scores on reading proficiency compared with Caucasian children, and they lag behind their peers in letter recognition and phonemic awareness at kindergarten entry (Reardon & Galindo, 2006).

These findings suggest that interventions focused solely on increasing Latino families' access to early care and education programs will not be enough to close the achievement gap at kindergarten entry. It is necessary to ensure that programs provide high-quality, culturally responsive, and linguistically appropriate practices to promote optimal development among Latino children that will help them be ready to succeed in school.

Building Partnerships with Latino Families

Decades of research have shown that family involvement in children's early care and education is positively related to children's social and emotional development and academic achievement (e.g., Barnard, 2004; Shannon, Tamis-LeMonda, London, & Cabrera, 2002). Greater family involvement and more active types of involvement are associated with better language, social, motor, and adaptive development and greater mastery of early basic school skills of their children (Marcon, 1999). Furthermore, it seems that the positive impact of family involvement has a protective effect, particularly among children from families with low socioeconomic status and with ethnic minority backgrounds (Jeynes, 2003).

Among Latino families, the degree of involvement in planning and coordinating services for their children with disabilities has been found to be lower than the involvement of Caucasian families (Sontag & Schacht, 1994), and they are less likely to participate in parent programs (Heller, Markwardt, Rowitz, & Farber, 1994; Shapiro & Simonsen, 1994). The lower degree of involvement also has been reported for families of typically developing Latino children.

This low involvement can be explained in part by difficulties in gaining access to and utilizing services, as previously described. Also, parents' views about the early education, early intervention, and social services systems are influenced by their previous experiences. Those views can create misunderstandings, and sometimes barriers, between families from culturally and linguistically diverse backgrounds and the professionals providing services to them. For example, as mentioned, immigrant families coming from areas with no system of services to support very young children with disabilities may not seek out those services in the United States.

Another explanation for the low involvement of Latino families is the difference in perceptions about the role of the parent and family and the role of the teacher and school in the education of their children. It has been found that Latino families tend to perceive that the role of the parent is to provide for the well-being of the child, ensuring that the child goes to school well fed, clean, and healthy so that he or she is prepared to learn; they also see their role as teaching their children morals, respect, and good behavior, whereas the role of the teacher and school is to support their children as they acquire new knowledge (Chavkin & Gonzalez, 1995; Espinosa, 1995; Trumbull, Rothstein-Fisch, Greenfield, & Quiroz, 2001). Latino families view teachers as important authority figures who deserve respect; thus, challenging or questioning what the teacher does in the classroom may be seen as disrespectful. Moreover, they may think that the teacher or other professional providing services to the family should know what is best for their children and may feel uncomfortable when asked to participate in the decision making, seeing it as an indication that the professional does not know his or her job. This attitude may be perceived by the teacher or service provider as lack of desire to participate or disinterest, but the family may be acting that way out of respect for the professional as "the expert." In situations in which parents do not agree with the teacher or service provider, they may remain silent or be reluctant to participate because of the fear that if they do complain, their child may lose the services he or she is receiving or may face negative consequences at school (e.g., maltreatment, discrimination).

Latino families, particularly those with low incomes, face a number of challenges that constitute barriers to their involvement in their children's education in the ways that are traditionally expected by early childhood programs and schools (e.g., parent–teacher conferences, parent teacher association [PTA] meetings, classroom volunteering). Some of those barriers are two or three work shifts per day, multiple jobs, inability to speak English, lack of transportation, and difficultly gaining access to child care (Martinez, DeGarmo, & Eddy, 2004).

This information suggests that an array of strategies tailored to address the specific needs of Latino families is necessary to increase their awareness and their level of involvement in their children's early education and early intervention programs. However, to be effective, the strategies should be designed based on a reconceptualized perspective about family involvement, one that incorporates the social and cultural contexts of Latino families and validates the many ways in which they support their children's education at home as well as in the program or at school.

Delgado-Gaitan (2004) proposed three major conditions for increasing Latino families' involvement: 1) connecting, 2) sharing information, and 3) staying involved. The first step in building partnerships with Latino families is reaching out to them (connecting). Face-to-face communication and telephone calls (in a language the families can understand) are usually more effective to connect with Latino families than sending written information (e.g., letters, fliers), even if it is available in Spanish. Personal relationships are usually very important for Latino families. When visiting or meeting with them, set aside time at the beginning to talk about family matters or important events that they would like to share with you before starting with the therapy or paperwork you need to complete. Establishing a personal relationship with the family will help build *confianza* (trust). If the family trusts you, they will not only feel more comfortable with you but will also be willing to follow your recommendations. If they do not trust you, they may say "yes" to you or show agreement, but they may not do what you recommend.

Establish a two-way mode of communication with the families (sharing information), so that Latino families receive information from the program or school about their children and are given the opportunity to share their perceptions with the teacher or service provider. Communicate program expectations about the level and ways in which families are expected to be involved, and find out about Latino families' expectations about the teacher and program roles.

Maintain the connection with the families (staying involved) by offering them opportunities to be involved that accommodate their needs and priorities. Allow them to participate on their own terms, sharing what they know and validating their knowledge about their children.

The implementation of these strategies requires an adequate institutional infrastructure that includes program policies, qualified personnel, and availability of materials such as the following:

- Hiring Spanish-speaking, preferably bicultural liaisons to conduct outreach and coordinate services.

- Collaborating with churches, *tiendas,* community colleges, ESL classes, and Latino and other community organizations for outreach services

- Hiring bilingual teachers or providers and trained interpreters

- Translating documents and information into Spanish

- Realizing that not all Latino parents are literate in Spanish and having a liaison or an interpreter available to answer questions and help parents understand documents and procedures

- Providing training for personnel on cultural and linguistic diversity

- Offering families transportation and child care

Conclusion

Module 3 discussed various approaches used in child rearing. Specifically, individualism and collectivism were presented as two distinct perspectives, with the acknowledgment that most families emphasize one perspective but incorporate elements of both when raising their children. The module explained child-rearing values and beliefs among Latino families, as well as their views on disabilities. The module also provided some suggested strategies for building partnerships with Latino families.

Key Ideas to Remember

- Different cultures raise their children in different ways. Values, beliefs, customs, traditions, and past experiences all play a part in how parents raise their children.

- Regardless of cultural backgrounds or experiences, there are some universal goals that all parents want to reach for their children.

- Reflecting on your own experiences and the way you were raised will help you better understand others' child-rearing practices.

- Do not make assumptions! Find out about the beliefs and practices of the families of the children you are working with and use that information when you plan early childhood classroom practices or early intervention services.

- Familism, *respeto,* and *educación* are child-rearing values shared by Latino families across national origins.

- Although Latinos share many common values, differences among Latino subgroups exist. Differences in sociodemographics, health status, and use of health and human services among Latino subgroups have been found to be equal to or greater than the differences among major ethnic groups.

- Some factors that may be related to differences among Latino subgroups include the family's degree of acculturation, country of origin, education level of the parents, and English proficiency.

- As in any ethnic or cultural group, it is possible to find different perspectives and points of view among individual families and, of course, among individual children.

Reflecting and Getting Ready for Change

Asking yourself the following questions will help you review the contents discussed in Module 3 and reflect on your current practices:

1. What were my parents' goals when they were raising me?

2. What are my goals or beliefs about raising children?

3. How are those goals similar to or different from the ones held by parents of children in my classroom (or in my early intervention program)?

4. In which ways do I emphasize individualism and collectivism in my classroom practices or early intervention services?

5. In what ways does my school or program emphasize individualism and collectivism in its policies and practices?

6. How much do I know about the values, beliefs, and practices of families of children in my classroom or program?

7. What strategies does my program use to build partnerships with the Latino families it serves?

References

Aparicio, E. (1998). *101 Spanish proverbs: Understanding Spanish language and culture through common sayings.* Chicago, NTC/Contemporary Publishing Group.

Arcia, E., Keyes, L., Gallagher, J.J., & Herrick, H. (1993). National portrait of sociodemographic factors associated with underutilization of services: Relevance to early intervention. *Journal of Early Intervention, 17*(3), 283–297.

Bailey, D.B., Skinner, D., Rodriguez, P., Gut, D., & Correa, V. (1999). Awareness, use, and satisfaction with services for Latino parents of young children with disabilities. *Exceptional Children, 65*(3), 367–381.

Barnard, W.M. (2004). Parent involvement in elementary school and educational attainment. *Children and Youth Services Review. Special Issue: Promoting Well-Being in Children and Youth: Findings from the Chicago Longitudinal Study, 26*(1), 39–62.

Bender, D.E., & Castro, D. (2000). Explaining the birth weight paradox: Latina immigrants' perceptions of resilience and risk. *Journal of Immigrant Health, 2*(3), 155–173.

Bowman, B.T., Donovan, M.S., & Burns, M.S. (2001). *Eager to learn: Educating our preschools.* Washington, DC: National Academies Press.

Chavkin, N.F., & Gonzalez, D.L. (1995). *Forging partnerships between Mexican American parents and the schools* (ERIC Document Reproduction Service No. ED 388489). Charleston, WV: ERIC Clearinghouse on Rural Education and Small Schools.

Delgado-Gaitan, C. (2004). *Involving Latino families in schools: Raising student achievement through home-school partnerships.* Thousand Oaks, CA: Corwin Press.

Espinosa, L.M. (1995). *Hispanic parent involvement in early childhood programs* (ERIC Document Reproduction Service No. ED 382412). Urbana, IL: ERIC Clearinghouse on Elementary and Early Childhood Education.

Greenfield, P.M., Keller, H., Fuligni, A., & Maynard, A. (2003). Cultural pathways through universal development. *Annual Review of Psychology, 54,* 461–490.

Greenfield, P.M., Trumbull, E., Keller, H., Rothstein-Fisch, C., Suzuki, L.K., & Quiroz, B. (2006). Cultural conceptions of learning and development. In P.A. Alexander & P.H. Winne (Eds.), *Handbook of educational psychology* (pp. 675–692). New York: Routledge.

Ginsberg, E. (1992). Access to health care for Hispanics. In A. Furino (Ed.), *Health policy and the Hispanic* (pp. 22–31). Boulder, CO: Westview Press.

Harwood, R.L., Miller, J.G., & Irizarry, N.L. (1995). *Culture and attachment: Perceptions of the child in context.* New York: Guildford Press.

Heller, T., Markwardt, R., Rowitz, L., & Farber, B. (1994). Adaptation of Hispanic families to a member with mental retardation. *American Journal on Mental Retardation, 99,* 289–300.

Hurtado, A. (1995). Variations, combinations, and evolutions: Latino families in the united states. In R.E. Zambrana (Ed.), *Understanding Latino families: Scholarship, policy, and practice* (pp. 40–61). Thousand Oaks, CA: Sage Publications.

Individuals with Disabilities Education Improvement Act (IDEA) of 2004, PL 108-446, 20 U.S.C. §§ 1400 *et seq.*

Jeynes, W. (2003). A meta-analysis: The effects of parental involvement on minority children's academic achievement. *Education and Urban Society, 35,* 202–218.

Keefe, S.E., & Padilla, A.M. (1987). *Chicano ethnicity.* Albuquerque: The University of New Mexico Press.

Keller, H. (2003). Socialization for competence: Cultural models of infancy. *Human Development, 46,* 288–311.

Kinukawa, A., Guzman, L., & Lippman, L. (2004). *National estimates of child care and subsidy receipt for children ages 0 to 6: What can we learn from the National Household Education Survey?* (Research brief). Washington, DC: Child Trends.

Lake, R. (Medicine Grizzlybear). (1990). An Indian father's plea. *Teacher Magazine, 2*(1), 48–53.

Magnuson, K.A., & Waldfogel, J. (2005). Early childhood care and educations: Effects on ethnic and racial gaps in school readiness. *The Future of Children, 15,* 188–196.

Marcon, R.A. (1999). Positive relationships between parent school involvement and public school inner-city preschooler's development and academic performance. *The School Psychology Review, 28*(3), 395–412.

Martínez, C.R., Jr., DeGarmo, D.S., & Eddy, J.M. (2004). Promoting academic success among Latino youth. *Hispanic Journal of Behavioral Sciences, 26,* 128–151.

National Center for Education Statistics. (2006). *The conditions of education 2006.* Washington, DC: U.S. Department of Education.

Ogbu, J.U. (1994). From cultural differences to differences in cultural frame of reference. In P.M. Greenfield & R.R. Cocking (Eds.), *Cross-cultural roots of minority child development* (pp. 365–391). Mahwah, NJ: Lawrence Erlbaum Associates.

Reardon, S.F., & Galindo, C. (2006). Patterns of Hispanic students' math and English literacy test scores. *Report to the National Task Force on Early Childhood Education for Hispanics.* Tempe, AZ: National Task Force on Early Childhood Education for Hispanics.

Rogoff, B. (2003). *The cultural nature of human development.* New York: Oxford University Press.

Romero, M.E. (1994). Identifying giftedness among Keresan Pueblo Indians: The Keres Study. *Journal of American Indian Education, 34,* 35–58.

Sabogal, F., Marín, G., Otero-Sabogal, R., Marín, B.V., & Perez-Stable, E.J. (1987). Hispanic familism and acculturation: What changes and what doesn't? *Hispanic Journal of Behavioral Sciences, 9*(4), 397–412

Shannon, J.D., Tamis-LeMonda, C., London, K., & Cabrera, N. (2002). Beyond rough and tumble: Low-income fathers' interactions and children's cognitive development at 24 months. *Parenting: Science and Practice, 2*(2), 77–104.

Shapiro, J., & Simonsen, D. (1994). Educational/support group for Latino families of children with Down syndrome. *Mental Retardation, 32*(6), 403–415.

Skinner, D., Correa, V., Skinner, M., & Bailey, D.B. (2001). Role of religion in the lives of Latino families of young children with developmental delays. *American Journal on Mental Retardation, 106*(4), 297–313.

Sontag, J.C., & Schacht, R. (1994). An ethnic comparison of parent participation and information needs in early intervention. *Exceptional Children, 60*(5), 422–433.

Sontag, J.C., Schacht, R., Horn, R., & Lenz, D. (1993). Parental concerns for infants and toddlers with special needs in rural versus urban counties of Arizona. *Rural Special Education Quarterly, 12,* 36–46.

Trumbull, E., Rothstein-Fisch, C., Greenfield, P.M., & Quiroz, B. (2001). *Bridging cultures between home and school: A guide for teachers.* Mahwah, NJ: Lawrence Erlbaum Associates.

Valdés, G. (1996). *Con respeto: Bridging the distances the between culturally diverse families and schools: An ethnographic portrait.* New York: Teachers College Press.

Vega, W.A. (1995). The Study of Latino Families: A point of departure. In R.E. Zambrana (Ed.), *Understanding Latino families: Scholarship, policy, and practice* (pp. 3–17). Thousand Oaks, CA: Sage Publications.

Zambrana, R.E. (Ed.). (1995). *Understanding Latino families: Scholarship, policy, and practice.* Thousand Oaks, CA: Sage Publications.

Recommended Resources

Ada, A.F., & Campoy, F.I. (1998). *Home–school interaction with cultural or language diverse families.* Westlake, OH: Del Sol Publishing.

This guide presents a transformative approach to home–school interaction with families from culturally or linguistically diverse backgrounds. In this approach, teachers recognize the potential of all individuals, regardless of age, gender, and ethnicity, to contribute to the transformation of their own lives and the lives of their family and community. Transformative education provides many opportunities for reaching providing connections between the home and school. The last two sections provide sample English and Spanish letters to parents on helping children to succeed in school, helping children develop language skills, developing home languages, preparing children to be good readers, home support for school success, and health tips.

Edelman, L. (2001). *Just being kids* [Videotape and booklet]. Denver: JFK Partners, University of Colorado, and Early Childhood Connections, Colorado Department of Education.

This videotape looks at the lives of six children and their families through six vignettes. Each story has its unique issues and discussion points. The videotape demonstrates how to collaborate with families to achieve meaningful goals for their children in everyday routines, activities, and places. It also comes with a facilitator's handbook.

Gonzalez-Mena, J. (1996). *Diversity: Contrasting perspectives* [Videotape]. Crystal Lake, IL: Magna Systems.

This videotape shows how relationships with parents can deepen when child care staff explore contrasting perspectives and spark dialogue. This videotape depicts variations on themes of independence, interdependence, and individuality in the delicate issues involved in day-to-day caregiving.

Gonzalez-Mena, J., & Tobiassen, D.P. (1999). *A place to begin: Working with parents on issues of diversity*. Sacramento: California Tomorrow.

This resource contains strategies for raising children who feel good about themselves and learn to appreciate and respect people who are different.

Hanson, M.J., & Lynch, E.W. (2004). *Understanding families: Approaches to diversity, disability, and risk*. Baltimore: Paul H. Brookes Publishing Co.

This research-based book provides suggestions for working effectively for all types of families whose children are at risk or have disabilities. In addition to giving an overview of demographics and family diversity, the book explains the influences of disability and other risk factors on family life and ways to help families facing these issues build resilience.

Harding-Esch, E., & Riley, P. (2003). *The Bilingual family: A handbook for parents* (2nd ed., rev.). New York: Cambridge University Press.

This easy-to-read book is a survey of the main issues for bilingual families, as well as deeper issues of language acquisition. The authors provide examples from real life to illustrate the issues.

Harry, B. (1997). *A teacher's handbook for cultural diversity, families, and the special education system*. New York: Teachers College Press.

This text helps future teachers become aware of traditional cultural stereotypes in special education and explains how to cast these stereotypes aside in order to work more effectively with students' families.

Lynch, E.W., & Hanson, M.J. (Eds.). (2004). *Developing cross-cultural competence: A guide for working with children and their families* (3rd ed.). Baltimore: Paul H. Brookes Publishing Co.

This book provides the reader with an introduction to issues surrounding working with families from diverse cultural, ethnic, and language groups. It describes the history, values, and beliefs of a number of cultural and ethnic groups living in the United States and provides recommendations for professionals providing intervention services.

Moore, S.M., & Perez-Mendez, C. (2003). *Cultural contexts for early intervention*. Rockville, MD: American Speech-Language-Hearing Association.

The increasing diversity of the U.S. population virtually guarantees that practitioners' caseloads will include children and families from a wide range of cultural and linguistic backgrounds. Because of a lack of training in this area, even practitioners who value culturally competent care and authentic family participation in early intervention may struggle to implement culturally sensitive practices. This program focuses on practical models and strategies to promote change in practice at several levels, and covers assessment and intervention practices across cultures (e.g., the use of cultural mediators, dynamic assessment).

Olsen, G.W., & Fuller, M.L. (2002). *Home–school relations: Working successfully with parents and families*. Boston: Allyn & Bacon

This book examines the nature of the contemporary family and its relationship to the school. It offers advice for educators on ways to develop strong home–school relationships and the importance of working relationships with their students. The book covers traditional family topics, as well as issues facing families today, such as poverty and domestic violence. In addition, diversity (cultural, racial, religious, and sexual orientation) is discussed throughout the entire book and even in a separate chapter. It also describes the techniques educators must use to understand the families from which their students come.

Valdés, G. (1996). *Con respeto: Bridging the distances between culturally diverse families and schools: An ethnographic portrait.* New York: Teachers College Press.

This book presents a study of ten Mexican immigrant families, describing how such families go about the business of surviving and learning to succeed in a new world.

Zambrana, R.E. (Ed.). (1995). *Understanding Latino families: Scholarship, policy, and practice.* Thousand Oaks, CA: Sage Publications.

This book presents an approach that centers on the strengths of Latino groups, the structural processes that impede their progress, and the cultural and familial processes that enhance their intergenerational adaptation and resiliency. The author discusses conceptual approaches to Latino families, programs, and practice, as well as policy implications. Salient topics include the economic well-being of Latino families, prospects for Latino children and adolescents, the adjustment of Central American refugee families, and Latino child and family health concerns.

Zhang, C., & Bennett, T. (2003). Facilitating the meaningful participation of culturally and linguistically diverse families in the IFSP and IEP process. *Focus on Autism and Other Developmental Disabilities, 18*(1), 51–59.

This article reviews literature regarding the involvement and participation of culturally and linguistically diverse families in the special education process. The author provides a summary of barriers to family participation and strategies for facilitating family participation. In addition, the author discusses issues and strategies for creating collaborative individualized family service plans (IFSPs) or individualized education programs (IEPs) with families from diverse backgrounds.

Supporting Language Development in Young Bilingual Children

NEW VOICES
N V
NUEVAS VOCES

Purpose

To increase participants' knowledge about language development in young bilingual children
To develop participants' skills for effectively assessing and supporting language development in young bilingual children

Objectives

- Understand the nature of language development and its relationship with thinking and culture

- Understand how second language learning occurs in young children

- Learn about effective strategies to support first and second language development in young children

- Understand cultural and linguistic considerations in the assessment of young bilingual children

The purpose of this module is to help early childhood professionals understand how young children learn a second language; the positive impact of bilingualism on children's development; the potential impact of home language loss on children's language, cognitive, and socioemotional development; common myths about second language acquisition; and how to support first and second language development among young bilingual children. Before discussing issues of second language development, however, it is helpful to review some important concepts about language development and its relationship with cognitive development and culture.

Young children begin to learn language at birth and continue learning language throughout their lives. Consequently, the language children learn first is the one spoken at home by the primary caregiver. They start learning language by getting familiar with the voices of those around them, the voices that give them a sense of comfort and security. Children learn to recognize familiar faces and the tones of voice associated with specific situations and will start communicating by responding with gestures (e.g., turning their heads toward the person who is talking or calling that person's name) or behaviors (e.g., crying, smiling). By age 2, children should be communicating using oral language; by age 5, most typically developing children are mastering the basic linguistic skills that allow them to communicate verbally with peers and adults. They like to talk, play with the language, ask questions, and invent stories, and they recognize positive and negative connotations of words and the power of words over people's behaviors. In the case of children whose home language is not English, much of this knowledge is usually acquired in their home language before they are enrolled in an early childhood program.

Language is a social fact; thus, language is learned based on need, purpose, and function. Children typically learn language when they need to communicate with others. Language facilitates social and interpersonal interactions; it is used to represent ideas about the world and connects these ideas and interactions, making them relevant to a specific social and cultural context (Halliday, 1978). Language learning, as other learning processes, occurs in the context of social interactions with adults and peers, who act as mediators between what the child knows and the new knowledge to be acquired (Vygotsky, 1962).

Language development is a continuous process that takes place everywhere. Whether at home, at the grocery store, or at the early childhood program, children continue learning language and using language to learn about the world around them. Language is a valuable instrument to develop thinking, organizing, and analyzing experiences, as well as to create new ones. Language and thinking are interrelated and reciprocal processes. Through language children grow intellectually, and that growth influences children's linguistic skills; improved language skills help children acquire more knowledge (Vygotsky, 1987).

Learning a language involves not only learning vocabulary and grammatical structures but also learning how language is used to communicate meaning in a specific cultural context. It also involves nonverbal behaviors and particular rules for the use of language—that is, which language expressions are appropriate to use depending on the person or situation. When children are exposed to an environment in which a language different from their home language is spoken, even their nonverbal behavior can be misinterpreted or misunderstood if it does not correspond to the expectations of caregivers in the new environment.

Language is also the communication tool through which children learn from their families about their cultural heritage and develop their sense of identity. Through language, parents teach their children values, beliefs, traditions, and ways of doing things that may be particular to their heritage group (Zentella, 2005). Without knowledge of their home language, children lose not only the connection with their families but also the opportunity to develop a sense of belonging to their heritage group and its history.

In summary, when young children come to an early childhood program, they bring all of the knowledge they have been accumulating over the first years of their lives. This knowledge about the world has been acquired through interactions with their families and communities that occurred in their families' primary language. When children's primary language is different than the language used in the early childhood program, their acquired knowledge about language as a communication system helps them in the process of learning a second language.

Second Language Development in Young Children

Yo siempre tuve en mi mente que mis niñas sean completamente bilingües, entonces quería que Karen pueda estar en un programa [preescolar] bilingüe, entonces, fuí a observar clases en diferentes escuelas, hablaba con diferentes maestras para ver cual era la situación. Como siempre las escuelas, los distritos escolares siempre quieren poner al niño en la escuela que esté más cerca de la casa, no? En este caso no estaba bien para mi hija, entonces yo tenía que convencerles y dándoles razones que esa aula específica es lo que ella necesitaba. Eso era en Tejas. Después, cuando ya aceptaron que participara en esa escuela [bilingüe], no hubo

I always had in my mind that my daughters would be completely bilingual, and I wanted Karen to attend a bilingual [preschool] program, so I went to observe classes at different schools, I spoke with different teachers to see what was the situation. Like always, the schools and school districts always want to enroll the child in the school that is closer to home, right? In this case, that was not the best for my daughter, and I had to convince them by giving them reasons why that specific class was the one my daughter needed. That was in Texas. Then, when they accepted that she could attend a bilingual school there were no problems. . . . Also, when

problemas. . . . También cuando estuvo en el kinder en Tejas estaba en una clase bilingüe, entonces seguimos con el español en la casa. Pero ya cuando vinimos aquí [a Virgina], Karen vino de la escuela hablando puro inglés, y lo que pasó es como a Linda, la de tres años, estaba en ese momento de desarrollar su idioma, entonces ella agarró lo que Karen, mi otra hija. Para mi es un poco frustrante porque yo quiero que hablen bien el español. Pero, Karen entiende todo y si tu le pides hablar o traducir, ella puede traducir asi de que ella puede traducir, pero ya su primera reacción no es en español. Pero Linda, no creo que va a poder, al menos que estemos en otra situación, con la familia de Marcos. Yo no creo que va a aprender muy bien [el español], va a entender porque entiende muy bien. Era muy común en Tejas esa situación de la gente que toda su vida estaban con sus abuelitos, sus padres hablándoles español y todo, pero salieron que no podían hablar, podían entender muy bien pero no podían hablar. Entonces, eso es lo que pienso que va ha pasar con Linda, y me da tristeza pues esa era siempre mi meta, que sean bilingües.

she was in kindergarten in Texas, she attended a bilingual class; then, we continued with Spanish at home. But when we came here [to Virginia], Karen came back from school speaking only English; what happened is that since Linda, my 3-year-old daughter was at that time developing her language, she got English from Karen, my older daughter. For me is somewhat frustrating because I want them both to speak Spanish well. However, Karen understands everything and if you ask her to talk or to interpret, she can interpret, but her first reaction is not to speak in Spanish anymore. But Linda, I don't think she will be able to do it [speak Spanish], unless our situation changes [and we live] with Marcos's family. I don't think she is going to learn [Spanish] well. She is going to understand. It was very common in Texas to find people who had lived all their lives with grandparents and parents speaking to them in Spanish, but they ended up not being able to speak Spanish; they could understand very well, but they could not speak it. So, that is what I think it is going to happen with Linda, and it makes me sad because my goal was always that they become bilingual.

—Sharon, Virginia

Sharon's story describes what happens to many parents whose home language is other than English and are struggling to support their children to become bilingual. It is evident that without the support from the school, it is much harder for parents to accomplish the goal of bilingualism for their children. This mother was not concerned about her daughters' ability to learn English; in fact, they were learning English without problems. Their home language was the one in jeopardy. Research with children of immigrant parents has shown a pattern of home language loss, with many children choosing to speak only English (Portes & Hao, 1998); this trend is particularly prevalent among the youngest children (Wong Fillmore, 1991). There are variations in how soon children of immigrants lose their home language, depending on national origins, but the bottom line is that English usage is alive and well among second-generation immigrant children. Therefore, research does not support the concern of many early intervention and educational programs that children of immigrants will not learn English.

The availability of dual language preschool and elementary education programs is limited in many communities around the country, particularly in states where the growth of the immigrant population is a recent phenomenon. Nevertheless, in programs where instruction is only in English, there are many things that teachers can do to support families so that their children develop both their home language and English (strategies to support first- and second-language development are included later in this module). Likewise, professionals working with children with disabilities who are growing up in a dual language environment should support parents' desire for their children to become bilingual. Karen, the girl in the preceding story, has a disability. She did well in a bilingual program, as her mother described.

How Children Become Bilingual

This section provides definitions and distinctions to explore the process by which children become bilingual.

Definition of Bilingualism

When is someone considered to be bilingual? The most common answer to this question is that a bilingual person is someone who can speak two languages. However, the answer is not that straightforward. There are many dimensions related to the process of becoming a bilingual person (Baker & Jones, 1998). Being bilingual involves abilities not only in speaking but also in listening, reading, and writing in two languages; however, it is rare to find a person who has the same level of ability in all aspects of each of the two languages. For instance, someone may be able to speak one language very well but use the other language for reading and writing. Or, a person might listen to and understand very well what is said in one language but use the other language for speaking. Nonetheless, individuals with different levels of ability in their two languages are still considered bilingual.

Bilingual individuals might use each of their two languages for different purposes and functions. A young child may use one language to speak to his or her parents and relatives and the other language to speak with the teacher or may use one language to express feelings and the other language to describe an academic task. As mentioned at the beginning of this module, language develops in social context and is used to establish relationships that facilitate the acquisition of knowledge. For bilingual individuals, this happens in two languages; furthermore, the totality of their life experiences happens in two languages. That is why it is very important that professionals give bilingual children opportunities to show what they know using their two languages. (Implications for practice and assessment are discussed in subsequent sections of this module.)

Distinctions Related to Bilingualism

Specific distinctions related to bilingualism include whether two languages are learned simultaneously or sequentially and whether the learning is additive or subtractive. Each topic is explored next.

Simultaneous or Sequential

Bilingual individuals learn their two languages either simultaneously or sequentially. A simultaneous process occurs when a child is exposed to two languages from birth or soon after; the sequential process happens when the child is exposed to the second language after the basic components of the first language have been established, at approximately age 4 (McLaughlin, 1984). Within the definition of sequential bilingualism, the term *early sequential bilingual* is used to refer to young children who started to learn English between 4 and 6 years of age in an early childhood program or kindergarten classroom (Peña & Kester, 2004); the term indicates that these children are learning a second language before they have mastery of their first language. This definition applies to the majority of young non–English-speaking children enrolling for the first time in U.S. early childhood programs, and these children are the focus of this module.

Most children who are considered sequential bilinguals may have been exposed to English to some extent before attending the early childhood program. For instance, young children may interact at home in a language other than English with their parents and in English with their siblings or may play with English-speaking children in their neighborhoods. Degrees of previous exposure to English result in variations in children's first language and English abilities at early childhood program entry. That is why it is recommended to identify these children's level of proficiency in both their first language and English and to use that information when planning classroom activities or interventions that support their development and learning.

Additive or Subtractive

The process of second language learning can lead to the mastery of two language systems or to the loss of the first language due to lack of support for its development and maintenance. This means that the process can be additive—if children develop and maintain their two languages—or subtractive—if the second language replaces the first language and, thus, children's abilities in their first language are reduced or completely lost (Cummins, 1994; Lambert, 1977). An example of additive bilingualism is a situation in which a child who speaks English, the majority language in the United States, learns a second language in school, which is encouraged and seen as a positive educational and social outcome. For this child, the English language is not in danger of being replaced by the second language, not only because it is the language spoken for people in the larger society but also because it is a language associated with school success and social prestige. Very different is the situation of a child whose family speaks a language other than English—that is, a minority language in the United States. This is the case of children of immigrant families, many Native American families, and families speaking "nonstandard" English dialects. Typically, a child who speaks a minority language is immersed in the second language (English) in school and in the community; the first language is ignored, not included in academic or social activities in the school or community, and restricted to the limited use within the family. Eventually, the child will not find a purpose to continue speaking his or her home or first language and might even feel embarrassed to be identified as someone from that language-minority community. This is an example of subtractive bilingualism. What are the outcomes of these two different experiences? The English-speaking child might eventually become proficient in two languages, whereas the child who spoke a minority language at school entry may learn English but lose his or her first language—and, with that, the opportunity to be proficient in two languages. Even worse, this child will be at risk of not acquiring an adequate level of proficiency in either language. In these examples, school experience had the effect of adding to a child's knowledge in one case and subtracting from a child's knowledge in the other.

Degrees of Bilingualism

Children who grow up in bilingual environments achieve different degrees of proficiency in each of their two languages. Theoretically, the levels of bilingual proficiency are comprised within a continuum that goes from partial or minimal bilingualism (in which the level of proficiency is higher in one of the languages than in the other) to balanced bilingualism (in which the level of proficiency is high in all language domains for both languages). Depending on factors such as the amount and quality of the language input and opportunities for using the language, children acquire different levels of proficiency in each of their two languages. Thus, they may be at different points of the bilingual proficiency continuum.

It is important to keep in mind that the process of second language learning does not happen in isolation and that it is influenced by many factors related to the child, family, early childhood setting, and community at large. For instance, individual characteristics such as child motivation, personality, and learning style can influence the speed and rate with which children learn a second language (August & Hakuta, 1997). Usually a strong motivator for children to learn a second language is their interest in interacting socially with peers and developing a sense of belonging to the group in the classroom and in the community. However, personality traits may influence the extent to which children initiate social interactions in order to make new friends or voluntarily participate in activities that involve speaking a new language. Teaching strategies that take into account differences in children's personalities and learning styles are more effective in supporting second language learning than those based on the assumption that all children learn in the same way.

Contrary to common belief, the most important family contribution to young children's second language learning is to help children develop and maintain their home language. This is particularly important for children attending an early childhood program in which instruction is provided only in English. Research has shown that among children growing up bilingually, a strong basis in the first language promotes school achievement in the second language and is important for ensuring that children do not become alienated from their families and communities (Sánchez, 1999; Tabors, 2008; Wong Fillmore, 1991). Furthermore, most experts support the idea that learning two languages at the same time does not cause confusion or language delays in young children and that teaching both languages actually facilitates English language learning (August & Shanahan, 2006; Bialystok, 2001).

Early childhood programs that offer opportunities for and encourage the development of children's home language as well as English send parents the message that using their home language is a desirable and beneficial activity that supports their children's development. How becoming bilingual is viewed and regarded in the early childhood environment and in the community at large are important considerations. If children are in an environment that welcomes them and embraces what they already know and bring to the classroom experience (i.e., their home language and culture), then they will be motivated not only to learn a new language and content knowledge but also to maintain their home language and use it as a learning tool.

What Children Gain by Becoming Bilingual

Studies conducted since the mid-1960s have shown positive effects of bilingualism on children's cognitive abilities, particularly those related to thinking about language forms (i.e., metalinguistic abilities). Bilingual children have been found to perform at a more advanced level than their monolingual peers in tasks such as comparing words by meaning (semantic dimensions), identifying repetition and contradictions in a statement, and judging the grammatical correctness of sentences in their two languages, as well as in a number of nonverbal capabilities (Bialystok, 1991; Hakuta, 1987; Galambos & Goldin-Meadow, 1990). Other areas of cognitive functioning that have also been found to be positively influenced by bilingualism are concept formation, reasoning by analogy, and problem solving (Bialystok & Majumder, 1998; see Lee, 1996, for a review). Previous knowledge of the different functions and rules of a language facilitates the process of learning a second language.

However, the positive cognitive consequences of being bilingual seem to be more evident among bilinguals who have an age-appropriate level of proficiency in both languages. High levels of bilingual proficiency are associated with cognitive advantages (Cummins, 2000). The association among advanced bilingualism (high proficiency in various dimensions of language ability across two languages—e.g., can speak, read, and write in two languages), cognitive ability, and academic performance has been demonstrated by studies showing that advanced bilinguals outperformed limited bilinguals (those with low proficiency in several dimensions of one language or low proficiency in both languages) and monolingual English-speaking children from the same national origin in standardized academic tests and grade point averages (GPAs) (Rumbaut, 1995). Also, first- and second-generation advanced bilinguals had higher achievement scores than their native-born English speaking peers (Portes & Rumbaut, 1996).

According to Cummins (2000), the quality of the learning environments and experiences to which bilingual children are exposed determines their level of bilingual proficiency and, thus, how much they can benefit from being bilingual. Based on this information, it seems reasonable to conclude that in order to help children take advantage of the benefits of bilingualism, early childhood professionals and parents should provide experiences that support children to reach advanced levels of proficiency in their two languages.

What Children Lose When They Lose Their First Language

As discussed previously, for sequential bilingual children the process of second language learning can lead to a partial or minimal proficiency in the first language or even its complete loss. It is not uncommon to find young bilingual children who can understand when someone speaks to them in their home language but cannot respond using that language. These children are receptive bilinguals; they have listening comprehension skills in their first language but have lost the ability to speak in that language. Most children who are receptive bilinguals may be less likely to learn to read and write in their first language than children who can communicate orally in their first language. Conversely, children who become literate in their first language are less likely to lose their ability to speak in that language.

First language loss is a gradual process that starts with a change in language preference, or language shift. Children will prefer to communicate in their second language and consequently will not continue developing their first language, which is known as first language attrition (Anderson, 2004). Children may retain abilities in some aspects of their first language while diminishing abilities in others. Eventually, children may completely lose their abilities in their first language. The probabilities of first language loss are higher among early sequential bilingual children who are introduced to the second language in early childhood programs or in the early elementary grades. A negative consequence of first language loss in the early grades is that the children do not develop high levels of proficiency in either language. The lack of use and support for developing the first language makes it difficult for them to achieve high levels of proficiency in that language, and the lack of a strong foundation in their first language makes it difficult for them to achieve high proficiency in English.

If children are in an environment that does not offer opportunities or encourage the use of their first or home language, they gradually start losing their abilities in that language and become monolingual English speakers. When children lose their home language, they are losing not only the positive effects of first language development on second language learning and the cognitive benefits of bilingualism; they are also losing the possibility of enjoying the support of their family and learning about their family traditions and heritage. The consequences can be devastating for children's socio-emotional development, affecting their identity and self-esteem. McGregor-Mendoza (2000) shared the testimonies of those affected by educational practices that explicitly discouraged and even punished children for using their home language in school, giving evidence of the negative impact of those practices on children:

> "Lady X", was grabbed and spanked by a teacher for speaking Spanish to the friend in front of her while on the playground one day, the incident made her wish she did not even know Spanish . . . As a result, Lady X forgot most of her Spanish and lost her culture as well (Connie J., unedited student writing).
>
> Well, then I was ashamed, and I also blamed my parents for not teaching me English. For a long time I lost my identity. I didn't want anyone to know that I could speak Spanish (Eva R., unedited student writing). (p. 34)

Myths About Second Language Learning

There are several common beliefs about second language learning that are not supported by research. Unfortunately, when professionals are unaware of these myths, their early intervention and early education practices may be based on false assumptions that negatively affect children's development and prospects for future school success. The following are some of the most common myths or misconceptions about second language learning, as discussed by Espinosa (2008), McLaughin (1992), and Sánchez and Thorp (1998).

Myth 1: Children learn second languages so quickly and easily that they suffer no traumatic consequences when immersed in an English-only caregiving or educational environment. The belief that young children acquire a second language quickly and easily leads teachers and other early childhood professionals to apply the "sink or swim" method, which means not offering support to young children while they are in the process of learning English. It is known that learning a second language is a process that takes several years (Saunders & O'Brien, 2006); in the early phases of learning a second language, young children may "look" proficient because they have learned a few phrases or even reached a level in which they can follow a conversation with peers and follow simple directions. However, they may not have acquired yet the English language skills necessary for understanding and performing more abstract and complex language tasks. Thus, early childhood teachers should plan instructional practices designed with the purpose of supporting second (English) language learning, not expect children to "get it" on their own.

Furthermore, socioemotional development is usually overlooked by the emphasis placed on having young language-minority children become proficient in English as soon as possible. The process of learning a second language is stressful and can even be painful for children who are learning not only a second language but also new sets of social rules and behaviors in an unfamiliar environment. How would you feel if you were left in a place in which you could not communicate with anybody and did not understand what was being said and done? Early childhood professionals need to go beyond the surface and be observant, providing young English language learners the social and emotional support they need.

Myth 2: The younger the child, the more skilled in acquiring a second language. There is a common assumption that the younger the child the quicker he or she will learn a second language. However, several reviews of the literature do not support this claim (e.g., Bialystok & Hakuta, 1994). Research in which children have been compared with adults in second language learning has consistently demonstrated that adolescents and adults perform better than young children. This is because older children and adults possess more advanced cognitive skills, which help them learn a second language at a faster rate than young children. Mature learners tend to make faster initial progress in acquiring grammar and vocabulary in the second language; younger learners tend to learn the phonological aspects faster, which means that they will have a native-like accent. Another aspect related to this myth is the fact that the language a young child needs to know in order to accomplish successful communication is a lot less complex than what is required from older children and adults. This, in addition to the native-like accent, contributes to the mistaken belief that young children become proficient in a second language sooner than older learners.

Myth 3: Learning a second language during the early childhood years will confuse the child and/or cause language delay or impairment. Brain-imaging research (e.g.,

Kovelman, Baker, & Petitto, 2008; Petitto & Kovelman, 2003) proposes that the human brain has the capacity to learn more than one language early in infancy, developing two differentiated linguistic systems that influence each other. Other studies have found that early bilingualism produces increased brain activity and neural tissue density that may have long-term positive effects on children's cognitive abilities (e.g., Mechelli et al., 2004). In addition, behavioral research indicates that children exposed to their first language and English in dual language programs acquire English language skills at an equivalent rate to those in English-only settings (Ramirez, Yuen, & Ramey, 1991). Furthermore, bilingual children may perform better than their monolingual counterparts in some tasks (e.g., Lindholm, 2001; Thomas & Collier, 2002).

These research findings indicate that young children are capable of learning two languages and that supporting first language development can actually facilitate the process of learning a second language. The more advanced the level of proficiency in the first language, the more it facilitates second language learning. A child's first language can act as a bridge, enabling him or her to participate more effectively in classroom or therapy activities while learning English.

Myth 4: Children have acquired a second language once they can speak it. A child who is proficient in conversational communication has not necessarily achieved proficiency in the more abstract and academic language needed to be successful in classroom activities. Children first acquire the language that allows them to engage in social interactions, such as playing with peers (e.g., "Pass me the ball," "I wanna play"), but they may not be able to follow instructions that involve more than one step, understand abstract concepts, or interpret what is explained in the language they are not fully proficient in yet. For instance, when after reading a book the teacher asks "Can you tell me why the main character of this story left his house?," English language learners may stay quiet or look distracted. Answering questions about a story is a task that requires a certain level of proficiency in understanding spoken language. As mentioned previously, it takes children several years to fully develop oral language skills in a second language (Genesee, Lindholm-Leary, Saunders, & Christian, 2006). (This topic is discussed in more detail in the sections "Developmental Phases of Second Language Learning" and "Components of Oral Language Development in Bilingual Children.)

Myth 5: All children learn a second language in the same way. Differences in learning styles are also reflected in the way children learn a second language. Some children learn best from listening, others from manipulating objects, and others from observing. It is important for teachers to present information to children in different ways and to be observant of children's responses to various stimuli. In addition to individual characteristics, there may be differences in learning styles that are related to the ways in which particular cultural groups use language. For example, as discussed in Modules 2 and 3, in some cultures people may use less spoken language to communicate than in others, and differences exist among cultural groups with regard to children's socialization. Family socioeconomic status also is related to the way in which children learn a second language; research has documented differences between low-income and middle-class families in terms of their communication styles and frequency of language interactions offered to children (e.g., Dickinson & Snow, 1987).

Developmental Phases of Second Language Learning

The information presented in this section corresponds to research conducted by Tabors (2008) with early sequential bilingual children attending a university early childhood program in the northeastern United States. After extensive observations of several second language learners' first contact with the English language in an early childhood classroom, Tabors proposed that second language learning among these children occurs in the following four sequential phases:

1. *Use of home language:* When children begin attending an early childhood program at age 3 or 4 years and are exposed for the first time to an environment in which a language other than their home language is spoken, a natural reaction is to try to communicate verbally using the only language they know, their first language. This may have happened to you if you have ever traveled to a non–English-speaking country and did not know the language spoken there. This phase usually does not last long, because children soon realize that their first language does not help them communicate in that environment; thus, they stop using their first language in the early childhood program. Furthermore, because the children do not know English yet, they stop talking all together in the early childhood program, getting into what is called a "nonverbal period" in the process of learning a second language.

2. *Nonverbal or observational period:* In this phase, children learning a second language are not communicating verbally in that language but are learning by listening and observing everything happening around them. During this period, children rely on gestures to communicate. It is very important to engage children at the beginning stages of learning English in all classroom activities, even if they are not speaking English yet, because they are using every opportunity to learn their second language. Moreover, offering classroom support in the children's first language should help them make sense of what is happening in the classroom and feel integrated to the group. There are no fixed rules about how long the nonverbal period lasts. Some children may stay in this phase for a month, whereas others may need several months or maybe a year. The story of Kristy, an early childhood teacher, illustrates this point:

I had a 4-year-old girl in my classroom, Julia, whose family was from Russia; they spoke only Russian at home. It was her first experience attending an early childhood program. I became concerned when after 6 months this little girl was not saying anything. She was quiet. I asked the parents if she was this quiet at home as well, and they told me that she was a "little parrot" at home, talking about what she had done in school, in fluent Russian. I was surprised, but still concerned because she will not talk in the classroom. I decided to visit this family in their home. We had a pleasant conversation, and Julia was there. The next day, when I saw her at the school and approached her to comment about my visit, she finally responded to me, in English!!! I was so happy that day!

Perhaps seeing her teacher at home made Julia feel more comfortable around the teacher and therefore more willing to try her beginning English language skills in the classroom. In addition, Julia was probably aware that she could not communicate verbally in English as her native English-speaking classmates did and might have been waiting to feel more confident about her skills before trying them out. As discussed previously, children's individual characteristics influence the process of learning a second language. Some children might be willing to take risks and try their new language earlier than others. However, what the teacher does to create a safe classroom environment where children feel comfortable trying their newly acquired second language skills plays an important role.

3. *Telegraphic and formulaic speech:* In this phase young children who are learning English start using one- or two-word phrases, such as naming people or objects and reciting the names of colors or shapes. They learn words that help them communicate basic needs (e.g., *bathroom, lunch*) and get into social interactions (e.g., *want play, mine*), which is called telegraphic speech. Little by little children begin using more complex language structures, starting with language chunks which are memorized phrases (e.g., "I don't like it," "I don't know," "Excuse me"), identified as formulaic speech. During this phase, it is easy to get confused and assume that a child is already proficient in English because he or she is using grammatically correct expressions in English. However, the child might be using memorized expressions instead of creating original sentences. Ernesto's story offers a good example of what occurs in this phase:

   Ernesto was 4 years, 8 months old, and had arrived in the United States with his parents 6 months before. He went with his parents to the pool by the club-house in the condominium where they lived. Ernesto knew some of the children there and would play with them, without using verbal communication. While at the pool that day, a child came and jumped in with an inflated boat that he "rode" by manipulating the wheel. At that moment Ernesto exclaimed loudly, "What a pilot!" and everybody celebrated his very precise and timely comment. Ernesto's mother who was observing and knew that he had not been speaking English yet, was very surprised by the child's sudden "fluency" in English. Once back at home, Ernesto turned the television on, and Mom went to the kitchen. A few minutes later, she heard "What a pilot!" coming from the television. She ran to the living room to see who said it. It was Johnny Quest, a cartoon character, riding his boat. Then, Ernesto's mother understood that he had memorized that phrase and had found the right moment to use it!

4. *Productive language:* Eventually, young bilingual children will start constructing original sentences in their second language. At first they may combine memorized phrases with new words they have learned (e.g., "I do a ice cream," "I want go outside"). The number of words children know in English (vocabulary) will gradually increase. Children learn how to pronounce them correctly (phonology), improve in their use of English grammatical structures (syntax), and learn the appropriate use of English expressions in different social situations (pragmatics). A discussion of how these processes unfold in each of these language domains is presented in the next section.

The previously described phases may not always occur in a linear, consecutive manner. For example, young children who are learning a second language may combine the use of formulaic speech with the beginning productive use of their second language. In addition, there are individual differences in the time that it takes children to move from one phase to the other. Early childhood professionals should remember all of these important considerations when preparing to support children in various stages of second language learning and to avoid misinterpretations of children's behaviors that can result in inappropriate referral to special education or other special services.

Components of Oral Language Development in Bilingual Children

Learning a second language involves the mastery of the various components of oral language development. This section discusses how semantics, phonology, syntax, and pragmatics develop in children growing up in bilingual environments.

Semantics: *Words and Their Meaning*

How young bilingual children learn new words and how they use them in context is essential information for planning instruction, assessment, and intervention. Children growing up in bilingual environments have a similar developmental trajectory of vocabulary learning as monolingual children (Patterson, 1998), and their vocabulary growth is generally similar to that of monolingual children *when the vocabulary sets from both languages are considered together* (Peña & Kester, 2004).

A language is a tool used to communicate experiences, feelings, and ideas—everything related to people's ways of life. The words in a language correspond to specific social, cultural, and historical contexts, as well as beliefs systems. Therefore, words describing objects, people, or events that are critical in one language may not even exist in another. There might be words for which a translation cannot be found in another language. When children are learning two languages, they are building two sets of vocabularies that are related to two distinct cultural contexts. Moreover, bilingual children may use each language for different purposes and for communicating with different people in different places; all of this determines which words they learn in each language. For instance, a child may know the names of colors (e.g., *red, blue, yellow*) in English but not in Spanish and may know the names of some foods (e.g., *frijoles, aguacate*) in Spanish and not in English.

During the early stages of second language learning, children may use both sets of vocabularies to communicate, "borrowing" words from one language when communicating in the other language if they do not have enough vocabulary in the target language—for example, saying, "El kitty blanco" [The white kitty] (Grosjean, 2001). Over the course of the primary years, most bilingual children successfully separate their languages. Exactly when this occurs varies as a function of timing and exposure to language-learning opportunities.

Phonology: *The Sounds of a Language*

Learning about phonological development in bilingual children helps professionals distinguish difference from disorder. Typically developing monolingual children acquire most of the phonemes—speech sounds—of their native language by age 5. Young bilingual children may face challenges pronouncing certain letters and words when the second language contains sounds that do not exist in their first language

(Goldstein & Iglesias, 2004). This applies particularly to sequential bilingual children, those learning a second language when the phonological system of their first language has been established.

As it happens with vocabulary, young bilingual children use knowledge from their two languages to respond to a specific task. This means that when confronted with sounds they do not know in the second language, children tend to substitute them with the closest sounds they know from their first language. For example, in the Spanish language the sounds of the /sh/ and /th/ do not exist; therefore, a Spanish-speaking child learning English may pronounce words with those sounds using the /ch/ for /sh/ and the /t/ for the /th/, such as saying "chine" for *shine*, "choose" for *shoes*, and "tenks" for *thanks*. Also, the phonological system of the first language can influence the phonological system of the second language. For instance, there are no Spanish words that begin with an /s/. Therefore, Spanish-speaking children learning English will pronounce English words with this form by adding the /e/ vowel to begin, saying, for example, "estate" for *state* and "esmile" for *smile*.

The level of difficulty in learning the speech sounds of the second language depends on the characteristics of the first language. For example, some English sounds may be challenging to learn for Chinese-speaking children, whereas other English sounds may be challenging for Spanish-speaking children. Despite these challenges, among the different components of language, phonology seems to be the one in which younger children learning a second language have an advantage over older children and adults. Young children are more likely to discriminate between and learn different speech sounds and therefore acquire a native-like accent in the second language. Children accomplish this through explicit teaching of the new sounds and opportunities to practice.

Syntax: The Grammatical Structure of a Language

In the process of acquiring a second language, children may apply grammatical rules of their first language to their second language, or they may have not completely learned the full extent or limitations of a rule in their second language and misapply it systematically. For example, "My pant blue is dirty" uses the Spanish grammar in which the noun always precedes the adjective (i.e., "Mi pantalón azul está sucio"). Notice that the noun *pants* is not pronounced with the ending *s*; that is because in Spanish an ending *s* indicates a plural.

By a gradual process of trial and error, children slowly succeed in establishing closer approximations to the system used by native speakers of the second language (Brown, 1994). Therefore, errors observed during this stage need not to be seen as signs of failure but, rather, as evidence of the children's learning process.

Pragmatics: The Social Rules in the Use of a Language

Simply speaking correct language forms is not enough to ensure communication. In addition to acquiring the appropriate vocabulary and grammatical structures in a second language, young bilingual children need to learn the social rules of the English language. They need to learn what to say, when to say it, and how to say it! Language expressions are related to history and culture. The social rules of language use are among the most difficult skills to master in a second language. For example, certain words and expressions may be appropriate to use with peers or friends in informal settings and inappropriate, rude, and even offensive when used with a teacher or another authority figure. Also, children may be accustomed to informal ways of communication and have difficulties finding the appropriate expressions to communicate in a more formal setting, such as the classroom. Communication styles are also an important part of the process of learning to communicate in a second language. There may be differences among cultural and ethnic groups in the way in which individuals organize their speech in oral communications. For example, not in all cultural or ethnic groups do individuals "go straight to the point" when answering questions or narrating an event. Martita's story in Module 3 illustrates this point. Teachers and other early childhood professionals need to be aware of and sensitive to all aspects involved in the process of learning a second language, and they should plan their practices taking these aspects into account.

Bilingual Code-Mixing

Children who are learning a second language often mix elements of their two languages—words, phrases, or clauses—in a conversation (Genesee, Paradis, & Crago, 2004). This is often interpreted by early childhood professionals and parents as a sign of a child's confusion and inability to distinguish between the two languages. In many cases, this concern leads professionals to recommend not supporting the child's first language development. Bilingual code-mixing is a common characteristic found in individuals who are learning a second language. They use their first language as a resource to complete the ideas they want to communicate. Whenever they do not know a particular word or expression in the second language, they fill the blank with words or phrases from their first language. However, code-mixing usually evolves to become a characteristic of the bilingual adult, who has reached mastery of the two languages and can speak exclusively in one of the languages with monolingual speakers (monolingual mode) or can mix the two languages when in a conversation with another bilingual person (bilingual mode) (Grosjean, 2001). Code-mixing is a common and typical phenomenon among bilingual individuals and should not be interpreted as an indication of confusion in children who are learning a second language. (To learn more about bilingual code-mixing see Genesee, Paradis, and Crago, 2006, and Zentella, 1999.)

Strategies for Supporting First and Second Language Development

As previously noted, adequate first language development is needed to facilitate second language development. Strategies to support both involve classroom organization, classroom activities, interactions with bilingual children, and family involvement.

Classroom Organization

How the classroom is organized and managed influences children's comfort level and provides an environment that is supportive of development and conducive to learning. There are certain characteristics of the classroom that are particularly help-ful for young bilingual children. For example, providing a space where children can go when they feel the need to be by themselves helps children who are learning a second language, who may at times be tense or tired and might want to be alone. The space can have a table with manipulatives or a quiet corner with pillows and books. Consistency in classroom routines is another strategy that is useful for English lan-guage learners because it helps them follow what is happening in the classroom, even when they cannot understand every word spoken by the teacher or other chil-dren. It helps them integrate with the group.

Classroom Activities

Balancing large-group activities with small-group activities and one-to-one interac-tions is recommended. Participation in small-group activities may be less threaten-ing than whole-class activities for children who are learning a second language, and children may feel more at ease when beginning to use the new words and phrases they are learning. Also, children learning a second language can greatly benefit from individual instruction with teachers and peers. In center-based programs, teachers should incorporate time to work individually with the bilingual children when plan-ning classroom activities.

Activities that promote inclusion and collaboration among children are also good opportunities to support language development in children learning a second language. When pairing English-speaking children with bilingual children, the teacher should plan the activities in advance so that children can accomplish two goals: learn En-glish and make friends. It has been documented that peer interactions may not help improve English skills in children learning English as a second language unless the interactions are embedded in activities intentionally prepared to support English language learning (Saunders & O'Brien, 2006).

Reading aloud is an activity that can provide excellent opportunities to support the various components of second language learning, particularly increasing English vocabulary, and to promote early literacy development. When selecting books to read aloud in a large-group activity, try to obtain copies of books in bilingual children's first language. Also, it is helpful to use predictable books, big books, and books with many illustrations. A strategy to help children who are learning English participate in the reading-aloud activity is to have someone read to them the book selected, in their home language, before the large-group reading activity. In this way, children who are at the beginning phases of learning English will be able to follow the story and build their English vocabulary. (For a more detailed description of how to con-duct an effective reading-aloud activity with children who are learning English, see Gillanders and Castro, 2007.)

Interactions with Bilingual Children

For early childhood professionals who are not bilingual, interacting with children who are learning English may be challenging, especially at the beginning of the pro-cess. Learning a few words in a child's first language helps to establish a positive relationship, communicating the teacher's or provider's interest in the individual child. This, along with a caring and warm attitude, supports children in facing their own challenges: being in an unfamiliar environment, in which they do not understand the language spoken (and perhaps even the way in which people behave) and what it is expected from them. Other specific strategies are discussed in the following sections.

Augment Verbal Communication

It is very important for professionals to be observant and follow closely children's phases of second language learning so that they can provide appropriate support. Using gestures, visual aids, and props, along with words helps to build vocabulary and increase comprehension. Some professionals have used sign language as a resource to communicate with children who are learning English. That can be a helpful strategy but only when 1) used with all children so that everyone in the classroom is learning sign language and it is not exclusively used with the bilingual children and 2) it is accompanied by verbal communication. The risk involved in this practice is not providing enough oral language input to the children, when that is precisely what they need the most—a lot of oral language input in both their first and second language. The goal is having them develop expressive language (speaking) as well as receptive language (listening comprehension) skills.

Talk to the Children During All Phases of Language Learning

Talk to the children who are learning English, even if they are not speaking in English yet or are going through a silent or nonverbal period. They are learning English at all times, using every opportunity provided to them. Also, if the children respond in their first language to a question or comment made in English, acknowledge their response, then model the response in English. Remember that bilingual children first develop their receptive language skills (understand what is being said) in the second language; therefore, they may understand more English than what they can produce.

Talk About Current Activities

Talking about what is happening at the present moment is also a useful strategy. This helps children understand and relate words with a situation or an event. Also, it is helpful to keep messages simple and repeat key words in a sentence.

Allowing bilingual children to speak their first or home language in the early childhood setting will not jeopardize the process of second-language learning. Phrases such as, "Don't talk to me unless you do so in English," or "In this classroom, we only speak English," send the message to the children that their home language and culture are not valued and, therefore, the children are not valued in that environment.

Allow Bilingual Children to Speak Their First Language

As noted, allowing bilingual children to speak their first or home language in the early childhood setting does not jeopardize the process of second language learning. Phrases such as, "Don't talk to me unless you do it in English," or "In this classroom, we only speak English," send the message to the children that their home language and culture are not valued. In turn, such comments send the message that the children are not valued in that environment.

Family Involvement

Creating a welcoming climate is the first step toward promoting families' participation in their children's early childhood program or getting them involved in their children's early intervention services. This can start with learning a few words in the families' home language, having interpreters available to help with communication, and hiring bilingual staff. The next step is encouraging families' active participation in activities, either with other children in the classroom (for center-based programs) or by partnering with the professional (in home-based programs). Inviting parents and/or other family members to share their language and culture demonstrates that their experiences and perspectives are acknowledged and valued. There are a variety of ways in which parents can have meaningful contributions. For example, they can participate in a reading-aloud activity, reading a story in their home language and teaching the whole class some vocabulary words in that language. Or, they can talk about a particular aspect of their culture, teach songs in their home language, and teach games that they used to play when they were children.

An important aspect of the involvement of families is what they do at home to support their children's development and learning. For language-minority families this can be challenging, when parents believe that supporting their home language can delay their children's English language learning process. Moreover, parents who are not proficient in English, and those who are proficient in English but want their children to develop and maintain their home language, may find themselves confronting the dilemma of not knowing which language to use with their children and feeling incompetent in supporting their children's development. Families need to be informed that supporting their children in their home language does not negatively affect English learning; furthermore, developing strong language skills in their home language helps children in some aspects of this process while supporting them in becoming bilingual. Parents should support their children in the language they are most familiar with, especially when reading to their children. It is difficult to ask questions or make comments and interpretations about a text or story read in a language that one does not know well. Sending books home in the children's first language and asking parents to read those books to their children reassures parents that reading in the home language is appropriate. To be sensitive to parents' different literacy levels in their first language, professionals can suggest that parents do a "picture walk"—that is, telling a story to their children using the pictures in the book. In addition to books, parents can be encouraged to teach their children songs, rhymes, and word games in their home language.

Assessment of Young Bilingual Children: Linguistic and Cultural Considerations

Appropriate assessment of bilingual children takes on particular significance. As Ortiz and García (1989) noted,

> The disproportionate representation of English language learners in special education reflects a general lack of understanding in our school systems of the influence of linguistic, cultural, and socioeconomic differences on student learning. Limited English proficiency is often misinterpreted as a disability, while a disability is sometimes misinterpreted as limited English proficiency. (Ortiz & Yates, 2002, p. 65)

The next sections explore this topic and other important assessment issues.

Prereferral Process

An effective prereferral process can reduce the number of inappropriate referrals to early intervention or special education services by helping to distinguish difficulties associated with second language learning from problems related to a disability. Before referring a child for an assessment because there is a suspicion that the child has a disability, the early childhood professional needs to gather information about the child's previous experiences, the parents' child-rearing beliefs and expectations about their child's development and learning, the child's current phase of second language learning, factors that influence second language learning, and classroom practices and supports offered to the child's second language learning, as well as to his or her developmental and educational growth. The following questions can help in this process (Cummins, 1984; Ortiz & García, 1989):

- How long have the child and his or her family lived in the United States?

- What is(are) the language(s) spoken in the child's home?

- Has the child been in an out-of-home care setting before?

- Are the activities or instruction compatible with the way that people from the child's culture acquire language and other cognitive skills?

- Do the activities or instruction build on the child's prior knowledge and experiences in his or her own family and community culture?

- Is language use in the classroom or therapy infused into activities that the child enjoys?

- Is the curriculum or intervention known to be effective with children from diverse cultural backgrounds?

- Is the curriculum or intervention known to be effective with bilingual children?

- Have the child's difficulties been validated?

    Is the concern shared by family members and other professionals interacting with the child?

Do difficulties occur in different settings?

Do difficulties seem not to be related to the child's personal characteristics (e.g., temperament, personality)?

Are difficulties not related to a change in the child's family life, classroom, or therapy environment?

- If the answer to one or more of the questions above is yes: Is there evidence of efforts to identify the source of difficulty that is affecting the child and to take corrective action (e.g., adapting or transforming instruction or the way in which activities are conducted during home visits or therapy sessions)?

The involvement of parents and other family members is critical to address the question of learning difference or disability. Families can help determine whether the child meets expectations of his or her group or there is a suspicion of a disability or delay. Also, knowledge of the child's community provides useful information about language use and cultural practices.

Conducting a prereferral process benefits children and families as well as the system. On the one hand, by avoiding misinterpretations, it gives bilingual children the opportunity to achieve to their highest potential. On the other hand, it ensures that resources are appropriately made available to support services for children who do have special needs. The prereferral process also has economic implications: Serving children within the context of a general education program is more cost effective than placement in early intervention or special education.

Determining Language Disability, Language Learning, or Language Difference

Differentiating between a temporary learning difficulty associated with acquiring a second language, a language difference associated with being bilingual, and a true language disability or disorder may be challenging for professionals who are not knowledgeable about how children learn a second language and how language develops in bilingual children. Furthermore, language use and communication style differences among cultural groups may need to be taken into consideration when determining if a child has a language disability. The following sections present some indicators to help distinguish language learning or language difference from language disability in bilingual children.

Developmental Milestones

Language disorders or disabilities are usually associated with delays or disorders in other developmental domains. If a child is not presenting delays in other areas of development, it is possible that the difficulty observed is related to learning a second language and not to a developmental disability. The child's parents or primary caregivers can provide valuable information by sharing whether they agree with the professional's concern about the child's development.

Nonverbal or Observational Period

As mentioned in previous sections, children may go through a nonverbal or observational period while learning a second language. Professionals who are not knowledgeable about second language learning may believe that these children are experiencing a language delay associated with a disability condition.

Preference for English

A previous section discussed the phenomenon of language loss in young bilingual children. When a child focuses his or her attention on learning a second language, thereby changing his or her language preference before competency in the first language is fully developed, arrested development or loss of proficiency in the first language may result. Therefore, assessment results typically indicate a low level of performance in both languages. This can lead the professional to believe that the child is having problems in the development of both languages, which can be taken as an indicator of a language disability.

Language Interference

As noted, the vocabularly development of children who are learning a second language goes through a period in which they may borrow words from the first language while communicating verbally in the second language. Also, they may use the grammatical structure of the first language with words from the second language while they are still learning the syntax rules of the second language. Therefore, evidence of first language interference in the English language samples is not necessarily an indicator of a language disability.

Receptive Language

When children are learning a second language, the receptive (listening) aspect develops first. If the child's receptive ability is typical in both languages, it is possible that the difficulty observed is not related to a disability.

Summary

In order to avoid misinterpretations of children's ability levels, early childhood professionals need to develop a good understanding of the process of second language learning. In addition, professionals should learn how the different components of language unfold in typically developing children growing up in bilingual environments. They also need to be aware of the potential similarities that can exist between second language learning and language impairment or disorder (Genesee, Paradis, & Crago, 2004).

Methodological Challenges

There are several challenges to conducting valid and reliable assessments with bilingual children. The six most common issues are as follows:

1. *Use of unfamiliar procedures:* When testing situations and environments are unfamiliar, children may feel intimidated or threatened and not perform at the highest level possible for them. This is particularly true when using standardized tests, which requires following a strict protocol (e.g., verbal interaction is restricted to the test script—no additional explanations are allowed), and when the assessment is conducted in a language the child cannot understand.

2. *Lack of appropriate norms:* Norm-referenced tests compare a person's score against the scores of a group of people who have already taken the same test (i.e., the norm group). Most standardized norm-referenced assessment instruments available have norms representing the experiences and belief system of the majority population (i.e., Caucasian, monolingual English-speaking children). Therefore, children who are not familiar with those experiences and are from families that may have different belief systems may fail when assessed with those instruments. Such failure can be mistakenly attributed to deficiency instead of to the use of a culturally biased assessment tool.

3. *Assessment only in English:* Assessing children's knowledge and abilities in a language in which they are not fully proficient may result in erroneous identification of developmental delays. Furthermore, children growing up in bilingual environments learn in different settings using both of their languages. Conducting an assessment only in English and not in the children's first language provides incomplete information about children's content knowledge and abilities. To address this challenge, some professionals use a screening method to identify children's dominant language and then proceed with the assessment in that language. This method does not completely solve the problem of getting only partial information about the child, as illustrated by the following professional's questions:

   I have a question about scoring an assessment given to a 4-year-old in Spanish. I use the Pre-LAS [Pre-Language Assessment Scales; Duncan & De Avila, 1986] as a screener for children whom the teacher says speak Spanish at home. If the child passes 80% or more of the items, I assess in English; less than 80%, I assess in Spanish using the TVIP [Test de Vocabulario en Imagenes Peabody; Dunn, Lugo, Padilla, & Dunn, 1986] and the Woodcock-Muñoz Language Battery [Woodcock-Muñoz Language Survey; Woodcock & Muñoz-Sandoval, 1993]. What do you do about a kid who fails the Pre-LAS (i.e., you assess in Spanish) and then he starts naming pictures in English about as good as any English-speaking kid his age? My first reaction is that once you start down the Spanish assessment course, the child can only get credit by giving you the words in Spanish. But, then, why did he fail the Pre-LAS?

   The answer to the questions posed by the professional in the vignette is twofold. The child may have learned the names of some objects in Spanish and others in English. In addition, the child may have not known the answer in English for the particular questions or items included in the Pre-LAS. The question about giving or not giving credit to a response in a language different from the language of assessment should be answered by determining the purpose of the assessment. If the purpose was to assess the child's content knowledge, then a correct response in either language should be accepted as correct. If the purpose was to determine the child's proficiency in Spanish, then an answer in English should be considered incorrect. For all assessments other than those to determine language proficiency level, situations such as this can be avoided by assessing the child in both the first and the second language.

4. *Use of translated versions of tests*: There are some tests available in languages other than English; however, for various reasons, they still may not be appropriate to use with children who are learning English as a second language. First, these tests may be a literal translation from the English, which does not solve the problem of cultural bias; furthermore, this can change what the item is intended to measure (e.g., a literal translation can change the level of difficulty of the specific item or question). Second, the tests may not take into account dialectal variations. A child may be assessed with a test that is translated in a dialect that is different from the dialect used at home. Third, the tests may have been normed on monolingual populations, which do not represent the experience of bilingual individuals speaking the same language. For example, if a test available in Spanish has norms based on the performance of monolingual individuals living in a Spanish-speaking country, the potential for cultural bias remains—in addition to the problems of comparing the performance of bilingual and monolingual Spanish speakers.

5. *Use of verbal standardized tests:* Language proficiency strongly relates to test performance. A typically developing child who is learning English as a second language is expected to obtain low scores on standardized tests in English for some time. Unfortunately, too often these children are placed in the position of taking these tests before they have acquired the necessary level of mastery in their second language.

Alternative Assessment Methods

For the previously mentioned reasons, the use of standardized norm-referenced tests with bilingual children has several limitations. Therefore, it is recommended that professionals use informal measures to obtain a more accurate picture of the child's knowledge and skills. Depending on the purpose of the assessment (e.g., planning classroom activities, determining eligibility for early intervention or special education services, providing information for program evaluation and accountability), informal measures can be used either to supplement or replace standardized norm-referenced tests. Some useful informal measures are as follows:

- *Analysis of language samples:* Language samples should be taken in both the first and the second language, in natural settings, and by a native speaker of each language. Language samples may include information about content knowledge, language use, vocabulary, syntax, and other components of language development, providing a comprehensive description of the child's linguistic capabilities.

- *Observations:* The professional conducting the assessment should observe the child's performance in natural settings outside of the testing situation (e.g., in the classroom, on the playground, at home).

- *Portfolios:* A review over time of the child's work done at home with parents, during therapy sessions or home visits, or in the classroom is usually a good source of information about the child's progress. It also can serve as a means for identifying areas of strength and those that need improvement.

- *Informal interviews:* Interviews should take place with family members, staff, and others who have regular contact with the child. As mentioned previously, the involvement of family members is critical to understanding learning difference or disability.

Guidelines for the Assessment of Bilingual Children

Guidelines for assessing bilingual children come from both legal requirements and professional recommendations. In this section, we present the federal requirements from the Individual with Disabilities Education Improvement Act of 2004 (IDEA 2004; PL 108-446) and recommendations from the National Association for the Education of Young Children (NAEYC; 2005) on this topic.

According to IDEA 2004, the materials and procedures used to assess children learning English as a second language must be selected and administered to ensure that they measure the extent to which the child has a disability and needs special education rather than measuring the child's English language skills. Education programs need to ensure that tests and other evaluation materials used to assess a child are

1. "Selected and administered so as not to be discriminatory on a racial or cultural basis" (IDEA 2004)

2. "Provided and administered in the child's native language or other mode of communication, unless it is clearly not feasible to do so" (IDEA 2004)

Furthermore, "no single procedure shall be the sole criterion for determining an appropriate educational program for a child" (IDEA 2004). Also, the law specifies that certain correspondence to parents must be in their native language to ensure their participation in assessment and intervention decisions.

After administering tests and evaluation materials, qualified professionals and the child's parents must determine if the child has a disability. A child may not be determined to be eligible under Part B if the determining factor for eligibility is the child's limited English proficiency and the child does not otherwise meet the criteria for a child with a disability (IDEA 2004).

In addition, the National Association for the Education of Young Children (NAEYC; 2005) published a set of recommendations and indicators of effective practice in the assessment of young English language learners that includes the following:

1. Assessment procedures should be appropriate for the identified purpose, using instruments that are culturally and linguistically appropriate. Whenever possible, bilingual children should be assessed in both English and their first language. Young children will be learning different things in each of their languages; conducting the assessment in both languages is the only way to make sure that the assessment is capturing what children know regardless of the language in which they learned the concepts.

2. Assessment procedures should include multiple methods of gathering information about the child's development, and should be conducted on an ongoing basis.

3. Assessment of young English language learners should involve more than one professional. At least one of these professionals should be bilingual (proficient in the child's first language) and bicultural (from the same cultural or ethnic group of the child).

4. The child's family should be included in the assessment process as they can provide information that will be critical in selecting assessment methods and interpreting assessment results.

5. Professionals conducting assessments of young English language learners should be knowledgeable about second language acquisition and trained to conduct assessments that addressed the specific characteristics of these children.

For more information on NAEYC's recommendations for the assessment of young English language learners, see NAEYC (2005).

Conclusion

This module presented information about bilingualism, including how it affects children's cognitive and social-emotional development and how second language learning unfolds in young children. Also, the module discussed strategies for working with young bilingual children that can be applied to different settings (e.g., home-based and classroom-based programs as well as therapy sessions), considerations for conducting linguistically and culturally appropriate assessments with bilingual children, and guidelines based on IDEA 2004 requirements and NAEYC recommendations.

Key Ideas to Remember

- Language and culture are two very closely related processes in children's development. When learning a new language, children are learning about new cultural perspectives and values as well. When losing a language, they are losing a connection to the culture with which that language is associated.

- Children growing up in bilingual environments learn by using the two languages to which they have access. Children learn everywhere, not only when they are in the classroom.

- Bilingualism can have positive effects in children's cognitive development, with advanced bilingual children having an advantage over their limited bilingual and monolingual English-speaking peers.

- The developmental sequence in learning a second language includes the following phases: 1) use of home language, 2) the nonverbal or observational period, 3) telegraphic and formulaic speech, and 4) productive use of the new language.

- Learning a second language involves all components of language. Children learn new words and their meanings (vocabulary), the sounds of letters and pronunciation of words in the new language (phonology), its grammatical structure (syntax), and the social rules for using the new language (pragmatics).

- Code-mixing (using two languages in the same phrase or sentence) occurs in the early stages of second language learning and usually becomes a typical characteristic of bilingual individuals.

- Effective strategies for working with young bilingual children take into consideration children's prior knowledge and experiences, the phases of second language acquisition, the importance of developing and maintaining the child's first language, and the role of families as partners to support their children's care and education and to inform the implementation of culturally and linguistically appropriate practices.

- Effective assessments of young children focus on individual strengths and uniqueness; are performance, process, and product based; are ongoing and occur in many contexts; are reflective, analytic, instructive, and useful; and involve the collaboration of children, their parents, their teachers, and professional specialists.

Reflecting and Getting Ready for Change

The following questions are intended to help you review the contents discussed in this module and reflect on the extent to which your current practices are meeting the needs of the bilingual children with whom you work.

1. How are language, culture, and thinking related?

2. How do children become bilingual?

3. What are the advantages of bilingualism?

4. Do I regularly observe and record information about the language development of children who are learning English?

5. Do I plan activities taking into account the language-learning phase of children who are learning English?

6. What strategies do I use to facilitate English learning among the children I serve?

7. What strategies do I use to support development and maintenance of the first or home language among the children I serve who are learning English?

8. What strategies do I use to involve language-minority parents in supporting their children's development?

9. What resources are available in my program to support implementation of culturally and linguistically appropriate practices with children who are learning English (e.g., bilingual staff, interpreters, professional development)?

10. Does my program's assessment procedures account for IDEA 2004 requirements and NAEYC recommendations?

References

Anderson, R.T. (2004). First language loss in Spanish-speaking children: Patterns of loss and implications for clinical practice. In B.A. Goldstein (Ed.), *Bilingual language development and disorders in Spanish-English speakers* (pp. 187–212). Baltimore: Paul H. Brookes Publishing Co.

August, D., & Hakuta, K. (1997). (Eds.). *Improving schooling for language-minority children: A research agenda.* Washington, DC: National Academies Press.

August, D., & Shanahan, T. (Eds.). (2006). *Developing literacy in second-language learners: Report of the National Literacy Panel on Language-Minority Children and Youth.* Mahwah, NJ: Lawrence Erlbaum Associates.

Baker, C., & Jones, S.P. (1998). Individual bilingualism. In C. Baker and S.P. Jones (Eds.), *Encyclopedia of bilingualism and bilingual education* (pp. 2–27). Clevedon, United Kingdom: Multilingual Matters.

Bialystock, E. (1991). Metalinguistic dimensions of bilingual language proficiency. In E. Bialystok (Ed.), *Language processing in bilingual children* (pp. 113–140). New York: Cambridge University Press.

Bialystok, E. (2001). *Bilingualism in development: Language, literacy, and cognition.* New York: Cambridge University Press.

Bialystok, E., & Hakuta, K. (1994). *In other words.* New York: Basic Books.

Bialystok, E., & Majumder, S. (1998). The relationship between bilingualism and the development of cognitive processes in problem-solving. *Applied Psycho-linguistics, 19,* 69–85.

Brown, D.B. (1994). *Principles of language learning and teaching.* (3rd ed.). Upper Saddle River, NJ: Prentice Hall.

Cummins, J. (1984). *Bilingualism and special education: Issues in assessment and pedagogy.* Clevedon, United Kingdom: Multilingual Matters.

Cummins, J. (1994). The acquisition of English as a second language. In K. Spangenberg-Urbschat & R. Pritchard (Eds.), *Reading instruction for ESL students* (pp. 36–64). Newark, DE: International Reading Association.

Cummins, J. (2000). *Language, power and pedagogy: Bilingual children in the crossfire.* Clevedon, United Kingdom: Multilingual Matters.

Dickinson, D., & Snow, C. (1987). Interrelationships among prereading and oral language in kindergarteners from two social classes. *Early Childhood Research Quarterly, 2*(1), 1–25.

Duncan, S.E., & De Avila, E.A. (1986). *Pre-Language Assessment Scales (Pre-LAS).* Montery, CA: CTB/McGraw-Hill.

Dunn, L.M., Lugo, D.E., Padilla, E.R., & Dunn, L.M. (1986). *Test de Vocabulario en Imagenes Peabody (TVIP).* San Antonio, TX: Pearson Assessments.

Espinosa, L. (2008). *Challenging commons myths about young English language learners* (FCD Policy Brief Advancing PK-3 No. 8). New York: Foundation for Child Development.

Galambos, S.J., & Goldin-Meadow, S. (1990). The effects of learning two languages on levels of metalinguistic awareness. *Cognition, 34*(1), 1–56.

Genesee, F., Lindholm-Leary, K., Saunders, W.M., & Christian, D. (2006). *Educating English language learners: A synthesis of research evidence.* New York: Cambridge University Press.

Genesee, F., Paradis, J., & Crago, M.B. (2004). *Communication and language intervention series: Vol. 11. Dual language development and disorders: A handbook on bilingualism and second language learning.* Baltimore: Paul H. Brookes Publishing Co.

Gillanders, C., & Castro. D. (2007). Reading aloud to English language learners. *Children and Families, 21*(3), 12–14.

Goldstein, B., & Iglesias, A. (2004). Language and dialectal variations. In J. Bernthal & N. Bankson (Eds.), *Articulation and phonological disorders* (5th ed., pp. 348–375). Boston: Allyn & Bacon.

Grosjean, F. (Ed.). (2001). *The bilingual's language modes.* Malden, MA: Blackwell Publishing.

Hakuta, K. (1987). Degree of bilingualism and cognitive ability in mainland Puerto Rican children. *Child Development, 58*(5), 1372–1388.

Halliday, M.A.K. (1978). *Language as social semiotic.* London: Edward Arnold.

Individuals with Disabilities Education Improvement Act (IDEA) of 2004, PL 108-446, 20 U.S.C. §§ 1400 *et seq.*

Kovelman, I., Baker, S.A., & Petitto, L.-A. (2008). Bilingual and monolingual brains compared: A functional magnetic resonance imaging investigation of syntactic processing and a possible "neural signature" of bilingualism. *Journal of Cognitive Neuroscience 20*(1), 153–169.

Lambert, W.E. (1977). Effects of bilingualism on the individual: Cognitive and sociocultural consequences. In P.A. Hornby (Ed.), *Bilingualism: Psychological, social, and educational implications* (pp. 15–28). New York: New York Academy of Sciences.

Lee, P. (1996). Cognitive development in bilingual children: A base for bilingual instruction in early childhood education. *The Bilingual Research Journal, 20*(3 & 4), 499–522.

Lindholm, K. (2001). *Dual language education.* Clevedon, United Kingdom: Multilingual Matters.

McGregor-Mendoza, P. (2000). Aquí no se habla Español: Stories of linguistic repression in Southwest schools. *Bilingual Research Journal, 24*(4), 333–345.

McLaughlin, B. (1984). *Second-language acquisition in childhood: Vol. 1. Preschool children.* Mahwah, NJ: Lawrence Erlbaum Associates.

McLaughlin, B. (1992). *Myths and misconceptions about second language learning: What every teacher needs to unlearn* (Educational Report 5). Santa Cruz: National Center for Research on Cultural Diversity and Second Language Learning, University of California.

Mechelli, A., Crinion, J.T., Noppeney, U., O'Doherty, J., Ashburner, J., Frackowiak, R., et al. (2004). Structural plasticity in the bilingual brain. *Nature, 431*(7010), 757.

National Association for the Education of Young Children. (2005). *Screening and assessment of young English language learners: Supplement to the NAEYC and NAECS/SDE Joint Position Statement on Early Childhood Curriculum, Assessment, and Program Evaluation.* Retrieved November 17, 2008, from http://www.naeyc.org/about/positions/pdf/ELL_SupplementLong.pdf

Ortiz, A.A., & García, S.B. (1989). A prereferral process for preventing inappropriate referrals of Hispanic students to special education. In A.A. Ortiz & B.A. Ramirez (Eds.), *Schools and the culturally diverse exceptional student: Promising practices and future directions* (pp. 6–18). Reston, VA: The Council for Exceptional Children.

Ortiz, A.A., & Yates, J.R. (2002). Considerations in the assessment of English language learners referred to special education. In A.J. Artiles & A.A. Ortiz (Eds.), *English language learners with special education needs: Identification, assessment, and instruction.* Washington, DC & McHenry, IL: Center for Applied Linguistics & Delta Publishing.

Patterson, J. (1998). Expressive vocabulary development and word combinations of Spanish-English bilingual toddlers. *American Journal of Speech-Language Pathology, 7,* 46–56.

Peña, E.D., & Kester, E.S. (2004). Semantic development in Spanish-English bilinguals: Theory, assessment, and intervention. In B.A. Goldstein (Ed.), *Bilingual language development and disorders in Spanish-English speakers* (pp. 105–128). Baltimore: Paul H. Brookes Publishing Co.

Petitto, L.A., & Kovelman, I. (2003). The bilingual paradox: How signing-speaking bilingual children help us to resolve it and teach us about the brain's mechanisms underlying all language acquisition. *Learning Languages, 8*(3), 5–19.

Portes, A., & Hao, L. (1998, October). E pluribus unum: Bilingualism and loss of language in the second generation. *Sociology of Education, 71,* 269–294.

Portes, A., & Rumbaut, R.G. (1996). *Immigrant America: A portrait* (2nd ed.). Berkeley: University of California Press.

Ramirez, J.D., Yuen, S.D., & Ramey, D.R. (1991). *Longitudinal study of structured English immersion strategy, early-exit and late-exit transitional bilingual education programs for language-minority children* (Final report to the U.S. Department of Education). San Mateo, CA: Aguirre International.

Rumbaut, R.G. (1995). The new Californians: Comparative research findings on the educational progress of immigrant children. In R.G. Rumbaut & W.A. Cornelius (Eds.), *California's immigrant children: Theory, research, and implications for educational policy* (pp. 17–70). La Jolla: Center for U.S.–Mexican Studies, University of California–San Diego.

Sánchez, S.Y. (1999). *Issues of language and culture impacting the early care of young Latino children.* Vienna, VA: National Child Care Information Center Publications.

Sánchez, S.Y., & Thorp, E.K. (1998). Policies on linguistic continuity: A family's right, a practitioner's choice, or an opportunity to create shared meaning and a more equitable relationship? *Zero to Three, 18*(6), 12–20.

Saunders, W.M., & O'Brien, G. (2006). Oral language. In F. Genesee, K. Lindholm-Leary, W.M. Saunders, & D. Christian (Eds.), *Educating English language learners: A synthesis of research evidence* (pp. 14–63). New York: Cambridge University Press.

Tabors, P.O. (2008). *One child, two languages: A guide for early childhood educators of children learning English as a second language* (2nd ed.). Baltimore: Paul H. Brookes Publishing Co.

Thomas, W., & Collier, V.P. (2002). *A national study of school effectiveness for minority language students' long term academic achievement.* Santa Cruz, CA: Center for Research on Education, Diversity and Excellence.

Vygotsky, L.S. (1962). *Thought and language.* Cambridge, MA: The M.I.T. Press.

Vygotsky, L.S. (1987). *The collected work of L.S. Vygotsky: Vol.1. Problems of general psychology (including the volume Thinking and Speech).* (N. Minick, Trans.) New York: Plenum.

Wong Fillmore, L. (1991). When learning a second language means losing the first. *Early Childhood Research Quarterly, 6,* 323–346.

Woodcock, R.W., & Muñoz-Sanoval, A. (1993). *Woodcock-Muñoz Language Survey.* Itasca, IL: Riverside.

Zentella, A.C. (1999). *Growing up bilingual.* Malden, MA: Blackwell Publishers.

Zentella, A.C. (Ed.). (2005). *Building on strength: Language and literacy in Latino families and communities.* New York: Teachers College Press.

Recommended Resources

Baker, C. (2001). *Foundations of bilingual education and bilingualism* (3rd ed.). Clevedon, United Kingdom: Multilingual Matters.

Bilingualism is presented in the context of national and local educational institutions, as well as social institutions. This textbook covers issues including second language acquisition, language testing, and language policy (e.g., California's Proposition 227).

Bialystok, E. (2001). *Bilingualism in development: Language, literacy, and cognition.* New York: Cambridge University Press.

This book explores the language and cognitive development of preschool-age bilingual children and provides a theoretical framework for interpreting the performance differences between bilingual and monolingual children. Topics examined include language acquisition, metalinguistic ability, literacy, and problem solving, as well as social issues faced by bilingual children.

Calderon, M.E., & Minaya-Rowe, L. (2003). *Designing and implementing two-way bilingual programs.* Thousand Oaks, CA: Corwin Press.

This book for school administrators, teachers, and parents explores the promotion of literacy in two languages, cross-cultural understanding, and high levels of academic achievement. It covers topics such as learning communities for dual-language teachers, professional development plans for specific dual-language programs, and parent involvement.

California Department of Education Press. (1998). *Assessing and fostering the development of a first and second language in early childhood: A training manual.* Sacramento: Author.

This manual is for training early childhood staff and parents to foster language development in children from diverse backgrounds.

California Department of Education Press. (1998). *Observing preschoolers: Assessing first and second language development* [Videotape]. Sacramento: Author.

This videotape is a good resource for learning how to distinguish, through observation, a true disability from just a difference in culture or language.

California Department of Education Press. (1998). *Talking with preschoolers* [Videotape]. Sacramento: Author.

This videotape is designed to help early childhood team members and family members develop skills and strategies for meeting the needs of culturally and linguistically diverse children.

Einkorn, K. (2001). *Easy & engaging ESL activities and mini-books for every classroom: Terrific teaching tips, games, mini-books & more to help new students from every nation build basic English vocabulary and feel welcome!* Jefferson City, MO: Scholastic.

This guide contains tips on preparing for new students who are learning English as a second language, ways to assess their needs and abilities, and guidelines for communicating with the students' families. This product, which meets Teachers of English to Speakers of Other Languages (TESOL) standards, contains vocabulary building thematic mini-books, games, and reproducible forms.

Freeman, Y.S., Freeman, D.E., & Mercuri, S.P. (2004). *Dual language essentials for teachers and administrators.* Portsmouth, NH: Heinemann.

This book provides the guiding principles and practices for successful dual language or two-way bilingual education and is based on the extensive research conducted by the authors. Topics relate to administration, teaching, curriculum, literacy, planning, and assessment. Each topic is illustrated with stories and specific examples drawn from many different bilingual classrooms.

Genesee, F., Paradis, J., & Crago, M.B. (2004). *Communication and language intervention series: Vol. 11. Dual language development and disorders: A handbook on bilingualism and second language learning.* Baltimore: Paul H. Brookes Publishing Co.

This book provides a synthesis of the current knowledge about typical bilingual and second language acquisition and disorders. Typical dual language development varies greatly from monolingual development, and professionals must understand these differences to successfully diagnose and treat dual language learners with language delays and disorders. The book discusses two types of dual language learners: bilingual children, who have learned two languages from infancy, and second language learners, who learn a second language after significant progress has been made in the first language.

Goldstein, B.A. (Ed.). (2004). *Bilingual language development and disorders in Spanish-English speakers.* Baltimore: Paul H. Brookes Publishing Co.

Professionals serve increasing numbers of Spanish-English bilingual children and need reliable assessment and intervention approaches for bilingual children with language disorders. This book, which focuses on children from 3 to 12 years of age, covers these topics by providing in-depth theoretical and practical information about developmental data, best assessment practices, and appropriate intervention approaches.

Gravelle, M. (2000). *Planning for bilingual learners: An inclusive curriculum.* Stokes on Trent, United Kingdom: Trentham Books.

This book offers a framework for teachers to include bilingual learners in their curriculum planning. It offers guidance from experienced teachers on ways to plan the curriculum so that it is accessible to all children in primary and secondary classrooms and in a range of curriculum areas.

Gregory, E. (Ed.). (1997). *One child, many worlds: Early learning in multicultural communities.* New York: Teachers College Press.

In this book, the authors review the spectrum of out-of-school language and learning practices (e.g., the role of caregivers, siblings, and community language classes). They also discuss ways in which teachers can act as mediators of a new language and culture.

Herrell, A.L., & Jordan, M. (2003). *Fifty strategies for teaching English language learners* (2nd ed.). Upper Saddle River, NJ: Prentice Hall.

This book gives 50 strategies to help English language learners understand content and improve their speaking, reading, writing, and listening in English skills. The strategies contain implementation instructions and are based on current standards, including Teachers of English to Speakers of Other Languages (TESOL) standards. The book provides information on nontraditional assessment methods such as anecdotal records, performance samples, and portfolios.

Kohnert, K. (2007). *Language disorders in bilingual children and adults*. San Diego: Plural Publishing.

This book for speech-language pathologists, advanced students in communication disorders programs, and clinical language researchers covers effective service delivery to bilingual children and adults with suspected or confirmed language disorders. The book addresses individuals of various ages, in numerous environments, and with diverse levels of first and second language proficiency.

Paradis, J. (2008). *Second language acquisition in children: Considerations for assessment* [Videotape and manual]. Rockville, MD: American Speech-Language-Hearing Association.

This book presents several important questions that need to be answered before assessing individuals who speak English as a second language. The included audio self-study provides an overview of the related research, focusing on language assessment in contexts where many languages are spoken and English is often the second language.

Peregoy, S.F., & Boyle, O.F. (2004). *Reading, writing and learning in ESL: A resource book for K–12 teachers* (4th ed.). Boston: Allyn & Bacon.

This book gives numerous strategies for promoting literacy and language development in English language learners from kindergarten through high school. It explains language theory as related to instruction and provides guidelines for motivating and involving English language learners. The book covers assessment, standards, sociocultural issues of language acquisition, education policy, and comprehension and metacognition.

Restrepo, M.A. (2007). *Effective interventions for English language learners* [Videotape and manual]. Rockville, MD: American Speech-Language-Hearing Association.

This videotape addresses the need to promote first language development in English language learners. It outlines intervention principles and factors for planning intervention programs and prioritizing goals for English language learners. This resource discusses vocabulary, grammar, story structure, phonemic awareness, and preventive techniques for the classroom and home.

Roseberry-McKibbin, C. (2003). *Assessment of bilingual learners: Language difference or disorder?* [Videotape and workbook]. Rockville, MD: American Speech-Language-Hearing Association.

This videotape provides information about typical second language acquisition, language differences versus disabilities in bilingual students, and ways to adapt standardized tests and use informal measures.

Tabors, P.O. (2008). *One child, two languages: A guide for early childhood educators of children learning English as a second language* (2nd ed.). Baltimore: Paul H. Brookes Publishing Co.

This book explains how teachers can accommodate the growing population of culturally and linguistically diverse children in their classrooms. It offers techniques to facilitate the natural progression of language acquisition in young children, explains ways to create a supportive classroom environment for English language learners, and stresses the importance of acknowledging students' home languages and cultures.

Tse, L. (2001). *"Why don't they learn English?" Separating fact and fallacy in the U.S. language debate*. New York: Teachers College Press.

This book examines the often cited, but poorly supported, claims that immigrants fail to learn English. It also explores the erroneous belief that immigrant communities cling to their heritage languages.

Working with Culturally and Linguistically Diverse Children

NEW VOICES
N V
NUEVAS VOCES

Purpose

To explore a variety of strategies and develop skills for working effectively with children who are culturally and linguistically diverse, particularly Latino children, in early education and early intervention services

Objectives

- Understand the concepts of culturally appropriate practices and multicultural education
- Explore a variety of strategies and develop skills for working effectively with children who are culturally and linguistically diverse, particularly Latino children, in early education and early intervention services

The nation's demographics are changing rapidly and, as a consequence, early childhood programs are increasingly serving more children and families who are culturally and linguistically diverse. Forty percent of the school population is from culturally and ethnically diverse groups, and some estimates anticipate that in 2039, children of color will make up more than 50% of the school population (Cochran-Smith, Davis, & Fries, 2004). In contrast, the National Center for Education Statistics reported that 86% of all teachers are Caucasian (Cochran-Smith et al., 2004). Children of immigrant families are largely contributing to the diversity in the population served by early childhood programs. Children in immigrant families are the fastest growing population group in the country. According to the 2000 U.S. Census, during the 1990s, "The number of children in immigrant families has expanded about seven times faster than the number in native-born families" (Hernández, 2004, p. 19).

Early childhood programs have a growing need for policies and practices that will ensure the health and education of the increasingly diverse population of children (Hernández, 2004). Higher education and professional development programs often do not include content to develop professionals' skills for working with children and families who are diverse, even though we know that a child's culture and language form an integral part of his or her development. Therefore, professionals must consider culture and language if they want to provide developmentally appropriate practices that meet the needs of all children (National Association for the Education of Young Children [NAEYC], 1995). Furthermore, state administrators of early childhood programs report challenges related to serving the growing Latino population given the lack of Latino or bilingual staff and the lack of sufficient preparation and training to serve these children and families (Buysse, Castro, West, & Skinner, 2004; Daniel & Friedman, 2005).

This module builds on the concepts, principles, and strategies presented in previous modules and discusses how to put that information into practice. We propose multicultural education as a framework for implementing culturally and linguistically appropriate early childhood programs. This approach allows integrating all of the ideas discussed so far. We begin by discussing the definition of *developmentally appropriate practices,* follow by providing information about the purpose and goals of multicultural education, as well as myths and misconceptions about multicultural education, and end by presenting strategies for taking a multicultural approach to serving young children and their families.

Diversity and Developmentally Appropriate Practices

I remember when my son was in preschool and they had a Thanksgiving meal for the children. One of the children in his class was a vegetarian. The teacher decided that the Thanksgiving meal would be centered around vegetable soup. It was great because all of the children were able to participate in the meal and no one felt left out.

—Nancy

Many of our children get into trouble because they just don't "act" like the other children. When my son was in first grade, his teacher called me at least once a week because he wouldn't sit in his seat and do his work. When I asked him, his answer was always, "But Mommy, I was helping Chas." We always taught our son that he and his sister should help each other. So, I could understand his need to help his friend. This way I could tell him what a generous person he was, but also help him to understand that in this case his teacher wanted to know what each of them could do on their own, then she would know how to help each of them do better.

—Tanisha

Since the late 1980s, early childhood professionals have agreed that practices should be developmentally appropriate. The Developmentally Appropriate Practices (DAP) guidelines developed by NAEYC and Bredekamp (1987) have been widely disseminated and used in early childhood programs across the country. In the early 1990s, however, concerns and questions were raised about who should determine what is developmentally appropriate and how it is determined. With the growing diversity among children in the United States, many of the concerns about DAP revolved around the research that was used to develop the guidelines, which was conducted mostly on children who were typically developing, Caucasian, and from middle-class families (Mallory & New, 1994). By failing to take into account the characteristics and lifestyles of children from culturally and linguistically diverse backgrounds, early childhood practices based on the DAP guidelines were not meeting the needs of a portion of the population. Furthermore, children from nonmainstream groups were at risk of being identified with developmental delays because of the mismatch between what the provider expected and what was considered appropriate in the child's familial and cultural contexts.

In 1995, the NAEYC published a position paper to help guide early childhood professionals on responding to the needs of children who are culturally and linguistically diverse. The foundation of the NAEYC position was

> For the optimal development and learning of all children, educators must accept the legitimacy of the children's home language, respect (hold in high regard) and value (esteem, appreciate) the home culture, and promote and encourage the active involvement and support of all families, including extended and nontraditional family units. (1995, p. 2)

This paper appeared at a time when professionals in the field of early childhood development and education needed guidance to gain a better understanding of the challenges as well as recommendations for working with young children in an increasingly multicultural and multilingual society.

Furthermore, Mallory and New (1994) and other researchers and professionals in the field questioned the definition of DAP, which did not consider cultural and language differences. It was through the leadership of NAEYC that the definition of DAP was revised to address the needs of children with cultural, linguistic, and developmental differences.

> What is usually missing is the discussion about social and cultural influences on a child's development and how families' beliefs, values, and practices around child development will influence the age at which certain abilities and behaviors appear and whether they are going to appear at all.

In most higher education programs that prepare early childhood professionals, students are still taught, and therefore become more familiar with, the concept of age-appropriate practice—developing an understanding of the typical ages in which children are expected to demonstrate specific abilities and behaviors. Likewise, professionals become familiar with, and value, the importance of focusing on an individual child's growth patterns, strengths, and experiences so that services are individually appropriate. What is usually missing is the discussion about social and cultural influences on a child's development and how families' beliefs, values, and practices around child development will influence the age at which certain abilities and behaviors appear and whether they are going to appear at all. Children are expected to develop their abilities in accordance with demands and expectations in the environment in which they grow up. Furthermore, focusing on the individual child using a cultural framework different from that of the child's family and cultural community may not be successful because it will lack understanding of the child's abilities.

Early childhood professionals can develop skills for gaining access to and using cultural and societal information about a child and his or her family. Integrating that sociocultural knowledge with what they already know about age-appropriate and individually appropriate services will enable professionals to provide developmentally and culturally appropriate services.

This section's opening quotes illustrate the integration of sociocultural knowledge into a child's educational setting. The first shows how a teacher was able to integrate one child's "differences" into a classroom activity to ensure the inclusion of all children. The second shows how a parent investigated the meaning behind her child's behavior and discussed with him reasons and expectations that were different in the classroom. With increased understanding of the importance of culture on a child's development, the field has redefined DAP to include not only age and individual appropriateness but also social and cultural appropriateness.

Multicultural Education

Education is still "separate but equal" in many areas of the United States decades after *Brown v. Board of Education* (1954) and the Education for All Handicapped

Children Act of 1975 (PL 94-142). Basic social attitudes are a barrier. Children are excluded from educational settings or opportunities based on physical accessibility and environment; lack of preparation and training among teachers and school or program administrators; resistance against inclusive programs by parents who fear that the education of their children will be compromised; lack of allocation of resources for equipment, renovations, and special therapies; and placement of children with disabilities in self-contained classrooms in some communities. Multicultural education has emerged as an approach to improve educational practices for all children and promote success among children most affected by different types of segregation and discrimination.

> Multicultural education is at least three things: an idea or concept, an education reform movement, and a process. Multicultural education incorporates the idea that all students—regardless of their gender and social class and their ethnic, racial, or cultural characteristics—should have an equal opportunity to learn in school. (Banks & Banks, 2007, p. 3)

Multicultural education is founded on the principles of freedom, equality, equity, and justice (National Association for Multicultural Education [NAME], 2006). It affirms that all children should have an equal opportunity to learn in school (Boutte, 1999) and that we have an obligation to prepare every child to live in an interdependent world (NAME, 2006). Therefore, a child's gender, economic status, culture, language, or abilities should not affect the quality of his or her care and education, and all children, regardless of their background, can benefit from multicultural education.

Equity and equality are values commonly held in the United States, but what do they really mean? Professionals attempting to put these values into practice may focus on treating every child equally. Some teachers or service providers are careful to ensure that every child is treated the same in order to be "fair." The principles of multicultural education challenge this notion and instead assert that professionals must give every child what that child needs in order to succeed. This means that the education process should be equitable, acknowledge and celebrate differences, accommodate children's different learning styles, and recognize what makes each child and family unique and value what they bring into the classroom or program. Professionals who have worked in early intervention and preschool services may find that their program values are compatible with those proposed by multicultural education proponents (e.g., emphasizing the importance of family-centered care, developing an individualized family service plan [IFSP] or individualized education program [IEP] for each child).

To assist professionals in understanding and implementing this approach, NAME (2006) defined multicultural education as follows:

> Multicultural education is a philosophical concept built on the ideals of freedom, justice, equality, equity, and human dignity as acknowledged in various documents, such as the U.S. Declaration of Independence, constitutions of South Africa and the United States, and the Universal Declaration of Human Rights adopted by the United Nations.... It values cultural differences and affirms the pluralism that students, their communities, and teachers reflect. It challenges all forms of discrimination in schools and society through the promotion of democratic principles of social justice.
>
> Multicultural education is a process that permeates all aspects of school practices, policies and organization as a means to ensure the highest levels of academic achievement for all students. It helps students develop a positive self-concept by providing knowledge about the histories, cultures, and contributions of diverse groups....

Multicultural education advocates the belief that students and their life histories and experiences should be placed at the center of the teaching and learning process and that pedagogy should occur in a context that is familiar to students and that addresses multiple ways of thinking....

To accomplish these goals, multicultural education demands a school staff that is culturally competent, and to the greatest extent possible racially, culturally, and linguistically diverse. Staff must be multiculturally literate and capable of including and embracing families and communities to create an environment that is supportive of multiple perspectives, experiences, and democracy. Multicultural education requires comprehensive school reform as multicultural education must pervade all aspects of the school community and organization.

Although multicultural education research and implementation have focused primarily on classroom practices, we believe that the values and goals of multicultural education can be applied to the early care and education of young children in center- or home-based programs. Likewise, they can be extended into everyday environments including home, work, and the community. Various authors have discussed the aims or goals of multicultural education (Banks, 1999; Boutte, 1999; Feinberg, 1996; Kendall, 1996; NAME, 2006; York, 1991). Following are multicultural education goals that we would like to highlight.

1. Teach children to respect others' cultures and values as well as their own

2. Help all children learn to function successfully in a multicultural and multiracial society

3. Develop a positive self-concept in those children who are the targets of racism or other forms of discrimination

4. Help all children positively experience their differences and their similarities

Multicultural education is designed to help children develop the knowledge, attitudes, and skills to participate in a democratic society. It promotes the freedom, abilities, and skills to cross ethnic and cultural boundaries to participate in other cultures or groups, sharing one's own perspectives and being enriched by those of others. It helps children break down the barriers of living with people different from them, including those with disabilities, making them feel welcome, respected, and included.

How to Implement a Multicultural Approach

In practice, multicultural education must be implemented broadly to create a democratic environment where all children will experience educational equality (Banks, 1999; NAME, 2006; York, 1991). Banks (2004) and Banks and Banks (2007) proposed the following dimensions of multicultural education to guide practice implementation.

- *Content integration:* Consistent infusion of ethnic and cultural content in all disciplines and any subject area. Teachers use examples from a variety of cultures to demonstrate ideas that are part of the curriculum.

- *Knowledge construction process:* Stories and experiences from the children's lives become part of the learning process. Teachers help children understand how knowledge is constructed as influenced by various perspectives including race, ethnicity, and social class.

- *Prejudice reduction:* Children develop positive attitudes toward different racial, cultural, and ethnic groups through lessons and activities. Teachers help children develop democratic attitudes, values, and behaviors.

- *Equity pedagogy:* Teaching styles are modified to facilitate the academic achievement of students from diverse groups (e.g., cooperative learning). Teachers use a variety of methods and approaches to ensure that all children, including those who are members of a minority status, succeed in academics.

- *Empowering school culture and social structure:* School/program culture is transformed to enable students of all backgrounds to experience equal status. The school structure and culture—such as labeling practices and teacher expectations—are designed to empower children of color, children with disabilities, children from low-income families, and children who might be vulnerable or be at a disadvantage.

A genuine multicultural approach to education should incorporate all these dimensions. A common limitation in many educational environments, however, is that programs and schools view multicultural education as just one of these dimensions—content integration—therefore limiting the breadth of the multicultural education approach. For example, teachers may set aside special days for celebrating heroes or holidays from various cultures, may include special lessons for understanding Native American culture, or may celebrate the Martin Luther King, Jr., holiday. This narrow implementation of multicultural activities is not the intention of the multicultural education approach and will not achieve the intended results.

Now look back at *An Indian Father's Plea* in Module 3 and deconstruct the story using these dimensions. How might the teacher implement a multicultural approach to create an environment that respects the child's culture and experience and supports the child's educational success?

With regard to *content integration,* how might the teacher use examples from a variety of cultures to demonstrate ideas that are part of the curriculum? For example, the teacher might implement counting or mathematics exercises that include familiar objects from Wind-Wolf's experience, such as sorting rocks, counting feathers, or counting beads on a beaded necklace or belt. How else might the teacher adapt the curriculum?

With regard to the *knowledge construction process,* how might the teacher create opportunities for stories and experiences from the children's lives to become part of the learning process? For example, the teacher might invite Wind-Wolf to share stories about different kinds of birds and their seasonal patterns as part of an activity teaching children about science and nature. Or, Wind-Wolf could share stories about the planets and moons when studying the solar system. What other opportunities might the teacher create?

For *prejudice reduction,* what types of activities might the teacher implement to promote positive attitudes toward different racial, cultural, and ethnic groups? For example, the teacher may provide an opportunity for the children to learn about similarities and differences focusing on hair color, texture, and length. The teacher may use this activity as a place for Wind-Wolf to share the meaning of long hair (masculinity) for Native American men. In addition, the teacher may be more vigilant in asserting him- or herself when prejudicial comments are made to counteract those comments. How else can the teacher promote positive attitudes about differences?

With regard to *equity pedagogy,* how might the teacher modify his or her teaching style to facilitate the achievement of children who are diverse? Perhaps the teacher can implement learning activities that emphasize Wind-Wolf's skills and allow him to demonstrate his skills, such as telling stories and "watch and study." What other modifications would better facilitate learning for children who are diverse?

Finally, regarding *empowering school culture and social structure,* how might the school or program create an environment where all families feel welcome and experience equal status? Perhaps the school or program can invite family members to have a greater role in determining school and classroom expectations and activities. What other actions could the school take to ensure all families experience equal status?

Myths About Multicultural Practices

Myths and misconceptions about multicultural education can be barriers to professionals' knowledge, attitudes, and skills for implementing multicultural practices. Different authors have discussed a variety of myths and misconceptions (Banks, 1999; Gómez, 1991). Four common myths will be examined because it is important to identify and dispel beliefs that can prevent you from understanding and using multicultural practices.

1. Multicultural practices emphasize how other cultures are different from the dominant culture.

2. Bilingualism is a liability.

3. Multicultural practices are only relevant in environments with children from diverse cultural and linguistic backgrounds.

4. Random and sporadic cultural activities make good multicultural practices.

Multicultural Practices Emphasize How Other Cultures Are Different from the Dominant Culture

This perspective focuses on differences and accentuates an "us versus them" polarity. On the contrary, the multicultural perspective does not promote one culture as better than another. Rather, it promotes the idea that children need to be aware of the uniqueness of their own culture when presented with information from other cultures and that children should learn about all cultural and racial groups.

Bilingualism Is a Liability

The influence of erroneous assumptions and misunderstandings has led to wide belief in the United States that bilingualism is too difficult and that second language learners will learn English more quickly if they stop using their first language. Myths and misconceptions about bilingualism have been used to convince professionals that an English-only approach to the child's education is the best option. Research findings, however, refute early conclusions about bilingualism as a disadvantage. In sharp contrast, as discussed in Module 4, studies showed that bilingualism is associated with higher levels of cognitive attainment (Bialystok, 2001; Gómez, 1991). The interrelatedness of first- and second-language proficiency suggests that the first language is an asset and a foundation on which to build the second language. An ideal early childhood setting will promote fluency in both first and second languages (Banks, 2004).

Multicultural Practices Are Only Relevant in Environments with Children from Diverse Cultural and Linguistic Backgrounds

A professional who holds this belief and works with a homogenous group of children would not include any multicultural activities into his or her program or classroom. A message from the director of a child care center illustrates this myth:

> We have been given a large number of brand new children's books and cassette tapes in Spanish. Presently, we only have one child who speaks Spanish, and we have kept a small group of books and tapes for him. Would your program have a need or use for these 30 books and 18 tapes? If so, let me know. If you do not need them, I could perhaps offer them to a program in another community that works with a fairly large Latino population. Let me know what you think. Thanks.

The multicultural approach assumes just the opposite—that all children need to experience diversity outside their immediate environment because our world is multicultural. Classrooms or environments where children are mostly from the same background should still provide a wide variety of materials and activities that teach about cultural and linguistic differences in our society as a whole. Multicultural practices are relevant for all children, not only for those who are not part of the mainstream.

Random and Sporadic Cultural Activities Make Good Multicultural Practices

Having a multicultural day once a year or setting aside time to celebrate holidays that are not usually a part of the curriculum (e.g., Hanukkah, Cinco de Mayo) is not enough when it comes to implementing multicultural practices. Celebrating holidays or recognizing heroes from non-Caucasian culture might be called the "contributions approach," the lowest level in the Approaches to Curriculum Reform (Banks & Banks, 2004); others have called this a "tourist approach." The second level, the "additive approach," adds some content and perspectives to the curriculum but does not change any of the structure of the existing curriculum. Changing the structure of the curriculum to incorporate the perspectives of the diverse groups is the third level, the "transformation approach." Finally, the "social action approach" not only transforms the curriculum, but also goes further by encouraging students to make decisions and take action to solve important social issues.

Multicultural materials and activities, selected on the basis of their developmental appropriateness, should be infused throughout the environment and the curriculum. When the professional introduces new materials and activities, he or she should always explain the cultural meaning and provide children with an opportunity to discuss and ask questions. Without a deeper understanding, children may be left feeling confused or thinking that other cultures are "weird."

Practicing Multicultural Early Care and Education

A multicultural environment will help children develop positive ideas about themselves and others through activities that encourage them to initiate conversations about differences. It is an environment that deals with issues of justice by encouraging critical thinking about bias and helping children develop the ability to stand up for themselves and for others. Furthermore, it is an environment where the professional carefully maintains the cultural continuity between home and the early childhood setting, and children can share and maintain their home culture and language.

For early childhood professionals who want to implement a multicultural approach, we recommend examining (and continuing to examine regularly, over time) the following.

- *Interactions with each individual child and his or her family members* with regard to demonstrating respect for individual and cultural differences and including the parents/family in the child's care and education; gathering information about family expectations and practices at home related to supporting the child's development; and integrating that knowledge into classroom or service provision practices

- *The types of activities for classroom- and home-based services* to engage the children, including activities that specifically focus on developing positive attitudes about racial, ethnic, ability, or gender differences and activities that focus on academic subjects (e.g., reading, mathematics, art) that incorporate the perspectives of different cultures

- *The physical environment* (e.g., room decorations, toys, dramatic play materials) to ensure that materials represent diversity and create positive self-images for the children in the room

- *Actions to promote the transformation of program or school culture and structure* to empower children of color, children with disabilities, or children from low-income families

Interactions with Children and Families

Early childhood professionals should regularly examine their everyday interactions with children and families to ensure respect for individual and cultural differences and inclusion of the parents or family members in the child's care and education. Professionals should

- *Respond to a child* when the child asks about differences and not avoid difficult subjects, including race, ethnicity, disability, language, and gender

- *Intervene when inappropriate comments or behaviors occur* to help children learn attitudes, values, and behaviors that support equality

- *Support each child* in maintaining his or her home culture and language (see Modules 3 and 4), including learning some words in his or her home language and responding to a child when the child is speaking his or her home language, even when professionals do not understand exactly what the child is saying

- *Try different approaches* tailored to the styles and preferences of each child and family to ensure all the children are being reached

- *Use stories and experiences from children's lives* to help them understand ideas and perspectives

- *Include parents and other family members* in activities to share traditions and practices from other cultures (see Module 3)

- *Elicit and respect parent and family input* into understanding their child's abilities

Resources and supports should be flexible, individualized, and tailored to the preferences and styles of the child and family (Sandall, Hemmeter, Smith, & McLean, 2005). Using various instructional styles can be particularly important for reaching children from diverse backgrounds. As covered in Module 3 with child-rearing practices, we know that developmental expectations and outcomes vary with cultural interpretations. It follows that methods of child care or education vary from one culture to the next. Practices in Caucasian, middle-class programs or schools in the

---

▓ A Mother's Story ▓

On the first day of school, a Mexican American mother and her 3-year-old daughter, who speak very little English, approach your classroom door. When the child's mother is introduced to her teacher, the child puts her arms around her mother's legs and starts crying, saying, "No, Mami. No, Mami." Some children stop and stare at her. A teacher tries to calm the crying girl and draw her into the classroom activities and asks the mother to leave the classroom. After 30 minutes, this young mother is still outside at the door unable to communicate her feelings, while listening to her daughter crying in the classroom.

For a minute, put yourself in this mother's situation. Imagine yourself in a foreign country where you do not speak the language and the natives do not speak English. Just satisfying your basic needs—getting a drink of water or finding a bathroom—can cause problems. Have you ever traveled in a country and confronted a language barrier? If so, what did you do? How did you feel when you read this story? If you were the professional in the preceding scenario, what would you do?

United States typically reflect the values and expectations of those providers and teachers. Activities may emphasize individual skills, for example. Games may often have children compete with one another.

Practices in other cultures challenge values and beliefs about child development in the United States. Caregivers might emphasize activities that teach children cooperative learning instead. For example, professionals in the Reggio Emilia approach (based on Italian cultural values and beliefs) do not teach children how to put their coats on but rather enjoy the opportunity to assist the children and encourage the children to help one another (Mallory & New, 1994). An activity that requires cooperation in order to be successful encourages children to seek out and cooperate with others.

As discussed in Module 1, the foundation for building a multicultural environment begins with professionals exploring their own culture, values, beliefs, and attitudes, as well as exploring the backgrounds of the children they serve. Knowing more about yourself will help you recognize what values and beliefs you have incorporated into your work and help you serve and be sensitive to the cultural and linguistic needs of children from diverse backgrounds.

Activities for Classroom- and Home-Based Services

Early childhood professionals should regularly examine the activities used to engage the children to ensure that they support multicultural practices. Professionals should include activities that specifically address differences and provide an opportunity for children to be exposed to and learn about different cultures and languages in a nonjudgmental way (Sandall et al., 2005). These activities allow the teacher or provider and children to learn about the cultural, ethnic, racial, and ability diversity of one another and the world in which they live. Children learn it is okay to be different, and they gain a sense of pride in their identity. They learn they do not have to leave their home culture at home when they come to the classroom. They do not learn that the dominant culture is somehow better than their home culture. These activities provide an opportunity for the teacher or provider to find out about the children's ideas about diversity and counter any misconceptions and stereotyping.

It is important that children learn about differences in a positive light. Your program or classroom can incorporate a variety of activities to teach young children about differences in race and culture. Try some of the examples from the list titled "Activities that Promote Racial and Cultural Awareness in Preschoolers" (p. 123).

Early childhood professionals should attempt to learn words and phrases in a family's preferred language (Hemmeter, Joseph, Smith, & Sandall, 2001).

Implementing multicultural activities in early care and education is not just about activities that promote racial and cultural awareness—it is about incorporating diversity into all activities. For example, a preschool teacher brought a multicultural approach to her literacy classroom, starting with a book about a young Mexican girl's experience at Christmas time.

Too Many Tamales

A preschool teacher has a class in which 20% of the children are Latino and 40% are deaf or hard of hearing and use cochlear implants. The classroom is a designated "literacy site" for the state. Each month, the teacher chooses one book to read with her class and incorporates the book's theme into the classroom activities. Motivated to bring multicultural practices to the classroom, this preschool teacher found creative ways to modify the existing literacy activities to incorporate cultural and linguistic differences.

First, the teacher decided that she would choose books that represented the cultural backgrounds of the children in her classroom. In December, the class read Too Many Tamales *(Soto, 1993), a Christmas story about a young Mexican girl. Knowing that the family members of her Mexican American students had limited English proficiency, the teacher obtained copies of the book in both English and Spanish so that all the children could take the book home and read it with their families.*

Second, the teacher modified the centers in the classroom to reflect the book and therefore to reflect Mexican culture. The dramatic play area included Mexican-style clothing, and a kitchen area included tortillas, tamales, and other Mexican play foods made out of felt. The reading center included books in both English and Spanish.

Third, the teacher wanted to encourage parent participation in the classroom. She invited one of the Mexican American mothers to come to the classroom to show the children how to make tamales. In early December, the mother came to the preschool classroom with tamales. The children gathered around the table and tasted the homemade tamales while the mother, through a bilingual interpreter, shared her recipe for making tamales.

It can be particularly challenging for some professionals to understand how to bring a multicultural approach to subjects such as math and science. When you begin to bring multiculturalism to everything you do, it will become easier. For example, an activity focused on counting skills, such as the sample activity plan in Figure 5.1, can incorporate a multicultural approach. The lesson not only helps the children understand the concept of counting, but also introduces the children to foods from different cultures. Likewise, a physical therapy session may seemingly be difficult to make multicultural, but as shown in Figure 5.2, it can be built into the overall approach.

Similarly, professionals can find ways to incorporate culturally and linguistically appropriate activities into services provided in the home. A professional must individualize services to meet a child's and family's needs and match their preferences and styles. Meetings should be scheduled in locations and at times that are convenient for the family. Parents and family members should be welcomed into the

Activity
Sorting and counting beans

Purpose
The children will practice counting and differentiating between similar items; the children will learn about different types of beans

Materials
1. Ten types of beans mixed together in a large container
2. A medium or large container for each group of children
3. An egg carton or cupcake baking pan for each group of children

Description
1. Pair the children or put them into small groups.
2. Pour a mixture of different types of beans into a container (one for each group).
3. Give each group an egg carton or cupcake baking pan.
4. Have children sort the beans, putting the same type together in each cupcake hole.
5. Ask the children how many types of beans they found in their container.
6. Ask the children what types of beans they found. Identify the types of beans that are unfamiliar to the children.
7. Ask, "What other types of beans do people eat?"
8. Consider inviting one of the parents to join the class and share a cultural dish made with beans.

Child participation/objectives
1. The children will sort beans.
2. The children will count the types of beans.
3. The children will try to identify the different types of beans.
4. The children will listen to information about types of beans and various cultures.

Supports
1. Provide individuals assistance with sorting, as needed.
2. Provide small-group assistance with counting, as needed.
3. Provide the names of beans that children cannot identify.
4. Provide information about various cultures and types of beans.

Figure 5.1. Sample activity plan for an activity focused on counting skills for children ages 4–5 years.

Activity
Physical therapy

Purpose
The child will develop leg muscles; the child will participate with family in recreational activities; the family will learn about community resources and how to gain access to those resources

Steps/description
1. Schedule a physical therapy visit with the family.
2. Tell the family that the community pool is a good place for physical therapy.
3. Plan ahead with the community pool for a time and place for a trained professional to conduct the physical therapy.
4. Tell the family to bring the child already dressed in a bathing suit.
5. Take the family to the community pool for the physical therapy.
6. Show the family how to get passes (e.g., fee, application) to the pool.
7. Conduct the therapy exercises at the pool with the parent or family members observing and participating.
8. Meet the family at the pool at the next therapy session. Encourage them to include other family members in the activity.
9. Conduct the therapy exercises at the pool with the parent or family members observing and participating.
10. Encourage the family to visit the pool on their own.
11. Check back to see if they were able to visit the pool successfully.

Child participation/objectives
1. The child will practice kicking and other leg exercises in the water.
2. The child will participate in a community activity.
3. The family will gain access to community resources.

Supports
1. Provide the child with the opportunity to strengthen leg muscles in the pool.
2. Provide the family with instructions/modeling regarding access to the community pool.
3. Provide the family with modeling of pool exercises.
4. Provide the family with support if they are unable to gain access to the community pool on their own.

Figure 5.2. Sample activity plan for a physical therapy session.

Activities that Promote Racial and Cultural Awareness in Preschoolers

Everybody Has a Color

Set out a number of nylon knee-high stockings (or skin paints or crayons) in various shades—browns, tans, yellows, reds. Encourage children to try them on their hands and arms or their legs and feet. Ask questions to help the children increase their awareness of skin color. For example, "Can you find a stocking that is the same color as your skin?" Or, "What color is that stocking you have on your arm?" Ask the children to "Try the _____ stocking. Is it lighter or darker than your own skin?" Tell the children no one's skin color is really white, pink, yellow, black, or red. Emphasize that skin color differences are interesting and desirable.

Hair Textures

Obtain samples of hair (wigs, dolls, hair salons, beauty supply shop), paste them onto index cards, put them in a box, and ask the children to identify each bit of hair. Talk about how hair has texture and curl. For instance, some people have fine hair, whereas others have coarse hair. Some people have straight hair, whereas others have curly hair. Talk about how people have different hair colors and lengths. With parent or guardian permission, take a photo of each child's face and make a collage of different hairstyles.

The New Voices ~ Nuevas Voces Guide to Cultural and Linguistic Diversity in Early Childhood
by Dina C. Castro, Betsy Ayankoya, and Christina Kasprzak
Copyright © 2011 Paul H. Brookes Publishing Co., Inc. All rights reserved.

early care and education of their child (Hemmeter et al., 2001; Sandall, et al., 2005). The following case illustrates these principles.

Katherine, an early intervention provider, is providing services for Mary, a 2-year-old Mexican American girl who has motor and language disabilities. Katherine decides to plan a home visit that incorporates many of the best practices she knows about early intervention and culturally and linguistically appropriate services.

Prior to the home visit, Katherine takes several steps to prepare: she thinks about how to incorporate the culture of the family—the home language of Spanish, the mother and siblings, and perhaps a family game—into the services for the child. In addition, she decides to practice some basic greetings and simple vocabulary in Spanish to be able to welcome the family and participate, at least minimally. She invites a trained interpreter from her program to assist with the meeting and talks at length with the interpreter about the purpose of the visit, a general idea of the activities planned during the visit, and the background of the child and family.

When Katherine and the interpreter arrive at the family home, their visit begins with Katherine greeting the family in Spanish and, through the use of the interpreter, talking to the mother about her current needs and concerns about Mary (trying to build trust or *confianza*). During the visit, the whole family is invited to share information about the family's everyday activities and about Mary's participation. Katherine asks the family to show her some of their typical family games, and during the games, she provides suggestions about how they can encourage and support Mary's participation in the games.

The Environment

Katherine's experience shows how a professional can build on the existing home environment to promote interactions that make children feel included and give them the opportunity to learn in their typical home and community environments. Early childhood professionals should regularly examine the physical environment and materials they use to ensure that the materials support multicultural practices. The physical environment (room decorations, toys, displays, books, music, art, food) should reflect the lives and interests of those within the program or classroom and also encourage knowledge and respect for individuals from various cultures in our own country and around the world.

Room decorations should not only incorporate all the races, ethnicities, cultures, and personal realities of the children in the program or school, but should also expose children to visual reminders of diversity that exists outside of the early childhood setting. Displays should include pictures of people of many colors, different forms of housing, various geographic settings from rural to urban, different family styles, and different expressions of cultural events and holidays (Sandall et al., 2005). Toys and books that reflect diversity in languages, races, ethnicities, cultures, and abilities should be available for children to explore. For example, if there are different languages (including sign language) in the program or classroom, then it is particularly important to include books, signs, and other materials in those languages. Children should be exposed to music, art, artifacts, and foods from different cultures and allowed freedom for exploring and cooperative learning.

Given that developmental outcomes vary with cultural interpretations, it follows that methods of child care or education vary from one culture to the next. Practices in other cultures may challenge the values and beliefs about child development prevalent in the mainstream. For example, a teacher might purposely select materials for the classroom that encourage cooperation and altruism, such as large building blocks that are too big for one child to carry alone.

Avoid using pictures, books, or objects that reinforce stereotypes when choosing materials for a program or classroom. Some professionals are unsure about including cultural diversity and end up having books and materials that just show animals. But choosing culturally and linguistically appropriate materials means finding books and materials that show people within cultural groups enjoying a range of customs and activities, living in a variety of settings, and belonging to a variety of socioeconomic groups, as well as single-parent families, two-parent families, and other styles of family composition. Do not confuse images of past ways of life of a group with its contemporary life or confuse images of people's holiday life with their daily lives. For example, Native Americans should not always be presented in traditional clothing, participating in traditional customs, and living in tepees. Look for bias or stereotypes in materials before selecting them. For example, books and materials should show women working inside and outside the home and men as caregivers. People of all races should be shown as professionals in positions such as doctors, teachers, and lawyers. Likewise, people of all races should be seen in service positions such as maids, gardeners, and cooks.

Furthermore, linguistic diversity can make an environment more welcoming to children and families and bring awareness and education to children who speak English. For example, a professional may want to use books and music in various languages. The physical environment might be labeled in two or more languages (see the English/Spanish Glossary of Familiar Words in the appendix at the end of this module), depending on the linguistic background of the children in the program.

Keep in mind that not all materials marked *multicultural* are good materials for your classroom or for the children you serve. It is essential that you find out about the children and families and about the cultural backgrounds and the communities in which they live. This information, together with guidance on selecting appropriate materials (see the Antibias Observation Checklist in Appendix C at the end of the book), will help you choose the materials that are right for the children and families you serve.

A preschool teacher with a diverse classroom, including Caucasian and African American children as well as Spanish-speaking Latino children, some of whom had hearing impairments, decided to enrich her classroom environment with multicultural materials, displays, and dolls. She bought posters, puzzles, and other materials showing children from various racial and ethnic backgrounds, as well as children with disabilities. She labeled classroom objects in both English and Spanish. She added an African American doll and a Latino doll in the housekeeping center and put a hearing aid on the Latino doll. Immediately, she noticed that all the children liked the new dolls. The children with and without hearing impairments wanted to play with the doll with the hearing aid. One day the teacher observed the children playing with the Latino doll with the hearing aid. One of the hearing kids started to put the infant in the sink for a bath, and one of the children with a cochlear implant said, "No, no, no, no!" The second child rushed to remove the hearing aid before the doll went into the bath water, adding, "This cannot get wet!"

Hints for Selecting Culturally and Linguistically Appropriate Materials

When choosing materials for your program or classroom, look at them closely to ensure that they are truly multicultural and appropriate. The following questions and ideas are from Santos and Reese (1999).

1. Does the publication, DVD, or CD take into account both implicit and explicit assumptions, beliefs, or values that are appropriate or potentially problematic for the receiving family?

2. Is the information presented in a format preferred by the receiving family?

3. Is the literacy level appropriate for the receiving family? Or, is the information presented in such a way that the family will find the material patronizing and insulting?

4. Are technical terms and jargon explained effectively? For example, does the publication include a glossary of frequently used terms?

5. Are the case studies, pictures, and graphics welcoming to the receiving family? For example, are diverse groups of people represented in the images? Do the images suggest a contemporary or nonstereotypical view of various families?

6. Find someone to help you review the translated material to prevent miscommunication and misunderstanding between you and the families with whom you work.

7. Develop excerpts, revise material, or present one chapter of a longer book or manual. (Be mindful of copyright issues.)

8. Develop companion brochures or guides to help parents apply concepts presented in a publication to their own situation.

9. Develop fliers that list related local resources or explain terms or jargon.

10. Remember: No single resource can address all of a family's needs, but in many cases, materials can be adapted to make them more useful.

Types of Bias to Look for in Books

Be aware of the types of bias that can be found in books when choosing culturally and linguistically appropriate materials. If you are familiar with the following types of bias (Sadker, Sadker, & Long, 1997), then you can recognize them in materials and avoid having biased books in your program or classroom.

- Linguistic bias: Culturally loaded terms (*black sheep, jew down*) or sexist language (*fireman, policeman, mailman*)

- Stereotyping: Stereotypes (e.g., ethnic, gender, socioeconomic status, religion) in storylines and illustrations

- Invisibility: Systematic exclusion of races, people of lower socioeconomic status, and so forth

- Imbalance: Simplifying complex issues or people by presenting limited, select information

- Unreality: Glossed-over discussion or unrealistic portrayal of issues (e.g., slavery, discrimination, prejudice, homelessness)

- Fragmentation: Information presented as unique occurrences rather than integrated in the text

School or Program Culture

What about the broader school or program culture? The most prepared teachers and service providers may find that the existing school culture or structure creates barriers to implementing a multicultural approach. Biases may exist in the very structure of the school or program, creating inequalities for children from races, cultures, or languages different from the dominant culture. For example, there may be policies regarding standardized testing, placing children into gifted or remedial programs, and tracking of students. There may be policies or procedures related to parent involvement, the calendar of holidays, and school or program activities, as well as hiring and training staff and programwide curriculum requirements.

Participating in transforming a school or program is the final step for a professional who wants to implement a multicultural approach. Banks (2004) talked about "empowering school culture and social structure." You can start by encouraging your school or program to create a mission statement and values that embrace

multiculturalism. Help identify existing policies that are barriers to multiculturalism and facilitate the change in order to create an environment that supports and
empowers all children, families, and professionals, regardless of race, ethnicity, language, and culture (Sandall et al., 2005). Policies that you may want to encourage
include the following.

- Hiring and retaining staff from different cultural and ethnic backgrounds

- Hiring and retaining bilingual staff

- Using multicultural or antibias curriculum

- Using multicultural materials such as books, dolls, and puzzles

- Using alternate authentic assessment methods

- Involving parents in the curriculum

Conclusion

This module discussed the concept of developmentally appropriate practices and how it has
changed to include cultural and linguistic diversity. The module talked about multicultural
education, its primary goals, and persistent myths that have prevented its full understanding. In
addition, it presented some strategies for incorporating a multicultural approach to child care
and education, including activities that promote cultural awareness and incorporate the home
culture and language. Finally, the module talked about transforming programs and schools so that
the culture and structure of these institutions support all children, regardless of race, ethnicity,
culture, language, gender, or disability.

Key Ideas to Remember

- Developmentally appropriate practices include not only age and individual appropriateness, but
  also social and cultural appropriateness.

- Multicultural education is both an idea and a process, founded on the principles of freedom,
  equality, equity, and justice, with the goal of creating institutions in which all children,
  regardless of gender, socioeconomic status, culture, language, or abilities, have equal quality
  of care and education and equal opportunities to succeed.

- Banks (2004) and Banks and Banks (2007) described five dimensions of multicultural
  education—content integration, knowledge construction process, prejudice reduction, equity
  pedagogy, and empowering school culture and social structure.

- There are persistent myths about multicultural education that prevent a full or accurate
  understanding and implementation of multicultural practices, including the ideas that
  multicultural practices emphasize how other cultures are different from the dominant culture,
  bilingualism is a liability, multicultural practices are only relevant in environments with
  children from diverse backgrounds, and random and sporadic cultural activities make good
  multicultural practices.

- Professionals who want to implement multicultural practices should continually examine and improve their interactions with children and families, the activities they use to engage children in the classroom- or home-based services, the physical environment where children receive services, and their program or school culture and structure.

Reflecting and Getting Ready for Change

To review the materials in this module, ask yourself the following questions:

1. Do I understand the purpose and goals of multicultural care and education?

2. What strategies have I learned that I can use to bring a multicultural approach to my services or teaching?

3. How might I build ongoing assessment of the physical environment, activities, and interactions with children and families into my work?

4. How will I change my behaviors and what activities will I incorporate into my practices to ensure that I am providing culturally and linguistically appropriate services to children and families?

5. How might I take action to assess and then improve the culture of the school or program in which I work? (See Appendix D at the end of the book.)

References

Banks, J.A. (1999). *An introduction to multicultural education* (2nd ed.) Boston: Allyn & Bacon.

Banks, J.A. (2004). Multicultural education: Historical development, dimensions, and practice. In J.A. Banks & C.A.M. Banks (Eds.), *Handbook of research on multicultural education* (pp. 3–29). San Francisco: Jossey-Bass.

Banks, J.A., & Banks, C.A.M. (Eds.). (2004). *Handbook of research on multicultural education.* San Francisco: Jossey-Bass.

Banks, J.A., & Banks, C.A.M. (Eds.). (2007). *Multicultural education: Issues and perspectives* (6th ed.). New York: Wiley.

Bialystok, E. (2001). *Bilingualism in development: Language, literacy and cognition.* New York: Cambridge University Press.

Bialystok, E., Craik, F.I.M., & Ryan, J. (2006). Executive control in a modified antisaccade task: Effects of aging and bilingualism. *Journal of Experimental Psychology: Learning, Memory and Cognition, 32*(6), 1341–1354.

Biles, B. (1994). Activities that promote racial and cultural awareness. *Family Child Care Connections, 4*(3), 1–4.

Boutte, G. (1999). *Multicultural education: Raising consciousness.* Belmont, CA: Wadsworth Publishing Company.

Bredekamp, S. (Ed.). (1987). *Developmentally appropriate practice in early childhood programs serving children from birth through age 8* (Rev. ed.). Washington, DC: National Association for the Education of Young Children.

Brown v. Board of Education, 347 U.S. 483 (1954).

Bullard, S., Carnes, J., Hofer, M., Polk, N., & Hernandez Sheets, R. (1997). *Starting small: Teaching tolerance in preschool and the early grades* [Videotape and book]. Montgomery, AL: Southern Poverty Law Center.

Buysse, V., Castro, D.C., West, T., & Skinner, M.L. (2004). *Addressing the needs of Latino children: A national survey of state administrators of early childhood programs. Executive summary.* Chapel Hill: University of North Carolina, FPG Child Development Institute.

Cochran-Smith, M., Davis, D., & Fries, K. (2004). Multicultural teacher education: Research, practice and policy. In J.A. Banks & C.A.M. Banks (Eds.), *Handbook of research on multicultural education* (pp. 931–975). San Francisco: Jossey-Bass.

Collins, T., & Hagerman, R. (1999). *Cultural resources for Mexican-American education.* Charleston, WV: ERIC Clearinghouse on Rural Education and Small Schools. (ERIC Document Reproduction Service No. ED438149)

Daniel, J., & Friedman, S. (2005). *Taking the next step: Preparing teachers to work with culturally and linguistically diverse children.* Retrieved September 28, 2008, from http://journal.naeyc.org/btj/200511/DanielFriedmanBTJ1105.pdf

Education for All Handicapped Children Act of 1975, PL 94-142, 20 U.S.C. §§ 1400 *et seq.*

Eggers-Piérola, C. (2002). *Connections and commitments: A Latino-based framework for early childhood educators.* Newton, MA: Center for Children and Families, Education Development Center.

Feinberg, W. (1996). *The goals of multicultural education: A critical re-evaluation.* Retrieved January 4, 2006, from http://www.ed.uiuc.edu/EPS/PESYearbook/96_docs/feinberg.html

Gómez, R.A. (1991). *Teaching with a multicultural perspective.* Urbana, IL: ERIC Clearinghouse on Elementary and Early Childhood Education. (ERIC Document Reproduction Service No. ED339548)

Gonzalez-Mena, J. (2001). Cross-cultural infant care and issues of equity and social justice. *Contemporary Issues in Early Childhood, 2*(3), 368–371.

Hemmeter, M.L., Joseph, G.E., Smith, B.J., & Sandall, S. (2001). *DEC recommended practices program assessment: Improving practices for young children with special needs and their families.* Longmont, CO: Sopris West Educational Services.

Hernández, D. (2004). Demographic change and the life circumstances of immigrant families. *The Future of Children, 14*(2), 17–47.

Hohensee, J.B., & Derman-Sparks, L. (1992). *Implementing an anti-bias curriculum in early childhood classrooms.* Urbana, IL: ERIC Clearinghouse on Elementary and Early Childhood Education. (ERIC Document Reproduction Service No. ED351146)

Jipson, J. (1991). Developmentally appropriate practice: Culture, curriculum, connections. *Early Education and Development, 2*(2), 120–136.

Kendall, F.E. (1996). *Diversity in the classroom: New approaches to the education of young children.* New York: Teachers College Press.

Mallory, B.L., & New, R.S. (Eds.). (1994). *Diversity and developmentally appropriate practices: Challenges for early childhood education.* New York: Teachers College Press.

Matthews, H., & Ewen, D. (2006). *Reaching all children? Understanding early care and education participation among immigrant families.* Washington, DC: Center for Law and Social Policy.

National Association for Multicultural Education. (2006). *Definition of multicultural education.* Retrieved July 11, 2006, from http://www.nameorg.org/resolutions/definition.html

National Association for the Education of Young Children. (1995). *Responding to linguistic and cultural diversity: Recommendations for effective early childhood education.* Washington, DC: Author.

Quiñones-Eatman, J. (2001). *Preschool language acquisition: What we know and how we can effectively communicate with young second language learners* (CLAS Technical Report #5). Champaign: University of Illinois at Urbana-Champaign, Early Childhood Research Institute on Culturally and Linguistically Appropriate Services.

Sadker, M., Sadker, D., & Long, L. (1997). *Gender and equality. Multicultural education: Issues and perspectives.* Boston: Allyn & Bacon.

Sandall, S., Hemmeter, M.L., Smith, B.J., & McLean, M.E. (Eds.). (2005). *DEC recommended practices: A comprehensive guide for practical application in early intervention/early childhood special education.* Longmont, CO: Sopris West Educational Services.

Santos, R.M., & Reese, D. (1999). *Selecting culturally and linguistically appropriate materials: Suggestions for service providers.* Champaign, IL: ERIC Clearinghouse on Elementary and Early Childhood Education. (ERIC Document Reproduction Service No. ED431546)

Schwartz, W. (1998). The schooling of multiracial students. New York: ERIC Clearinghouse on Urban Education. (ERIC Document Reproduction Service No. ED425249)

Soto, G. (1993). *Too many tamales.* New York: G.P. Putnam's Sons.

Stern-La Rosa, C.M. (2001). *Talking to children about diversity: Preschool years.* Retrieved June 16, 2004, from http://www.adl.org/issue%5Feducation/hateprejudice/Prejudice3.asp

Trueba, E.T., & Bartolone, L.I. (2004). *The education of Latino students: Is school reform enough?* New York: ERIC Clearinghouse on Urban Education. (ERIC Document Reproduction Service No. ED410367)

Vold, E.B. (Ed.). (1993). *Multicultural education in early childhood classrooms.* New York: National Education Association.

York, S. (1991). *Roots and wings: Affirming culture in early childhood programs.* St. Paul, MN: Redleaf Press.

Recommended Resources

Books and Videos

Artiles, A.J., & Ortiz, A.A. (2002). *English language learners with special education needs: Identification, assessment, and instruction.* Washington, DC: Center for Applied Linguistics.

This book describes the challenges involved in identifying, placing, and teaching English language learners with special education needs. Because many of these learners are placed inappropriately, this book guides educators on meeting their individual needs. It describes model programs and approaches, including early intervention programs, assessment methods, parent–school collaboration, and native and dual language instruction.

Baker, C. (2000). *The care and education of young bilinguals: An introduction for professionals.* Tonawanda, NY: Multilingual Matters.

This is a great introduction for professionals working with children who are bilingual, such as speech-language pathologists, doctors, psychologists, counselors, teachers, and special needs personnel. The book addresses the nature of children who are bilingual, everyday language use of bilinguals, children as interpreters, dialects and bilingualism, home and school relationships, bilingual classrooms, language delay and language disorder, and assessing bilingual children with special needs.

Ballenger, C. (1998). *Teaching other people's children: Literacy and learning in a bilingual classroom.* New York: Teachers College Press.

A teacher describes her experience teaching Haitian children in an inner-city preschool. The author struggles to find the academic strengths of children whose parents do not read them bedtime stories or otherwise prepare them for school in ways that are familiar to her. The author uses research to explore how teachers who listen closely to children from other cultures can understand the approaches to literature that these children bring with them to school. This book focuses on classroom behavior, concepts of print, and storybook reading, challenging many widely held assumptions and cultural perspectives about early childhood education.

Banks, J.A. (2000). *Cultural diversity and education: Foundations, curriculum, and teaching* (4th ed.). Boston: Allyn & Bacon.

This textbook provides a strong background in the conceptual, theoretical, and philosophical issues in multicultural education. It is designed to help preservice and in-service educators clarify the philosophical and definitional issues related to pluralistic education, derive a philosophical position, design and implement effective teaching strategies that reflect ethnic and cultural diversity, and prepare sound guidelines for multicultural programs and practices. This book describes ways to institutionalize educational programs and practices related to ethnic and cultural diversity. The scope of this edition has been broadened to include a focus on gender, disability, and giftedness.

Banks, J.A., & Banks, C.A.M. (2007). *Multicultural education: Issues and perspectives* (6th ed.). New York: Wiley/Jossey-Bass Education.

This handy reference is designed to help present and future educators acquire the concepts, paradigms, and explanations needed to become effective practitioners in culturally, racially, and language-diverse classrooms and schools. The sixth edition reflects current and emerging research, concepts, and debates about educating students from both genders and from different cultural, racial, ethnic, and language groups.

Barrera, I., Corso, R.M., & Macpherson, D. (2003). *Skilled dialogue: Strategies for responding to cultural diversity in early childhood.* Baltimore: Paul H. Brookes Publishing Co.

Skilled Dialogue is a field-tested model for respectful, reciprocal, and responsive interaction that honors cultural beliefs and values. This book helps practitioners learn the importance of cultural competence, improve their relationships with the children and families they serve, and better address developmental and educational goals.

Boutte, G. (1999). *Multicultural education: Raising consciousness.* Belmont, CA: Wadsworth.

This text examines multicultural issues from early childhood through elementary school, high school, university, and the workplace. Testing and parenting issues are examined, along with areas of multiculturalism, including ethnicity, religion, exceptionality, socioeconomic status, and gender. Institutional and individual discrimination are both explored.

Brice, A.E. (2002). *The Hispanic child: Speech, language, culture, and education.* Boston: Allyn & Bacon.

This book addresses the issues and struggles of school-age children who are Hispanic. This book is a good resource for clinicians and educators working with a bilingual caseload because it helps them understand and interact with their bilingual students and provide appropriate services.

Cordeiro, P.A., Reagan, T.G., & Martinez, L.P. (1994). *Multiculturalism and TQE: Addressing cultural diversity in schools.* Thousand Oaks, CA: Corwin Press.

Schools are facing challenges of increased racial and ethnic diversity, recognition of gender inequality, and a change in demographics of the American family. This book address the barriers of prejudice and discrimination that must be overcome to ensure an equitable, accessible, and high-quality education for all students. The book provides activities and approaches that can be used to broaden awareness, understanding, and communication. It promotes incorporating the philosophy of total quality education (TQE) with multicultural teaching in positive and supporting ways.

Delpit, L.D. (1996). *Other people's children: Cultural conflict in the classroom.* New York: The New Press.

Lisa Delpit suggests that many academic problems of minority children are the result of miscommunication and inequality in schools.

Derman-Sparks, L., & the A.B.C. Task Force. (1998). *Anti-bias curriculum: Tools for empowering young children.* Washington, DC: National Association for the Education of Young Children.

This resource shows early childhood educators how to examine biases and learn how they influence children. It offers ways to reduce, handle, or even eliminate biases and how to create an antibias environment that is developmentally appropriate.

Gay, G. (2000). *Culturally responsive teaching: Theory, research, and practice.* New York: Teachers College Press.

Geneva Gay makes a convincing case for using culturally responsive teaching to improve the school performance of students of color who are underachieving.

Genesee, F. (1994). *Educating second language children: The whole child, the whole curriculum, the whole community.* Cambridge, United Kingdom: Cambridge University Press.

Through an integrative approach to second language education, this book covers a wide range of issues affecting the academic and social success of language minority children. It deals not only with second language development, but also with whole child development. It addresses the entire curriculum, rather than focusing on language instruction. It also examines the role of the school, family, and community.

González, M.L., Huerta-Macías, A., & Tinajero, J.V. (2002). *Educating Latino students: A guide to successful practice.* Lanham, MD: The Scarecrow Press.

Today's teachers and administrators are in an influential position to reach Latino students and provide them with the education they need to succeed. This book discusses ways to create a supportive school culture and exemplary practices for educating Latinos from early childhood throughout high school.

Gonzalez-Mena, J. (2008). *Diversity in early care and education: Honoring differences.* New York: McGraw-Hill.

The author explores the rich diversity encountered in programs and environments for young children, including those serving children with special needs. The book emphasizes the practical and immediate concerns of early childhood professionals and family service providers.

Howard, G.R. (1999). *We can't teach what we don't know: White teachers, multiracial schools* (Multicultural Education Series). New York: Teachers College Press.

Gary Howard engages his readers through a journey of personal and professional transformation. He looks deeply into his own identity to discover what it means to be a culturally competent Caucasian teacher in racially diverse schools. This book offers a healing vision of the future of education in pluralistic nations.

Mangione, P.L. (1995). *Infant/toddler caregiving: A guide to culturally sensitive care.* Sacramento, California Department of Education.

This guide is used in conjunction with a four-module video training course for providers of family and center child care. The videotapes cover caregiving techniques for a specific area of care, and the guides provide extensive and in-depth coverage of a topic. This guide helps caregivers find ways to support the early development of infants and toddlers by becoming sensitive to the role of children's home culture and language.

Kendall, F.E. (1996). *Diversity in the classroom: New approaches to the education of young children.* New York: Teachers College Press.

Frances Kendall addresses many aspects of antibias education, from the stages of child development to strategies for educating parents, focusing particularly on the teacher's role as an agent of change. Kendall promotes teachers' self-awareness and provides guidelines for setting up multicultural environments and curricula.

Mallory, B., & New, R. (Eds.). (1994). *Diversity and developmentally appropriate practices: Challenges for early childhood education.* New York: Teachers College Press.

This book discusses various issues surrounding diversity, inclusion, and appropriate early educational practices.

Reyes, M.L., & Halcón, J.J. (Eds.). (2001). *The best for our children: Critical perspectives on literacy for Latino students.* New York: Teachers College Press.

Leading authorities and scholars lend their individual voices to a single, urgent issue—literacy for Latino students.

Trawick-Smith, J. (2003). *Early childhood development: A multicultural perspective* (3rd ed.). Upper Saddle River, NJ: Merrill/Prentice Hall.

This book takes a multicultural approach to development in children from birth to age 8, with expansive coverage of children with special needs. Diversity is incorporated into case studies and examples that provide future teachers with a hands-on guide to how children develop, how children's skills develop, and how that development should inform sensitive, successful teaching practice.

Vold, E.B. (Ed.). (1993). *Multicultural education in early childhood classrooms.* New York: Teachers College Press.

This book provides a rationale for multicultural education and serves as a manual for teachers. It includes activities and strategies for teaching preschool and primary-age children from a multicultural perspective.

Children's Books Addressing Diversity

Ada, A.F. (1999). *Mediopollito/Half-Chicken.* Las Vegas: Sagebrush Press. (Ages: 4–8)

This story retells the traditional folktale about how Half-Chicken became a weathervane. Half-Chicken goes to Mexico City to see the court of the viceroy and along the way helps the stream, the fire, and the wind. They return the favor when the viceroy's cook tries to turn him into chicken soup. Finally, the wind blows Half-Chicken to safety atop a palace tower where weathercocks have stood on their only leg, seeing everything that happens below and pointing whichever way their friend the wind blows. This story is told in a flavorful colonial Mexican setting.

Ada, A.F. (2002). *I love Saturdays y domingos.* New York: Atheneum. (Ages: 5–8)

Saturdays and Sundays are special days for the child in this story. On Saturdays, she visits Grandma and Grandpa, who come from a European American background, and on Sundays—los domingos—she visits Abuelito y Abuelita, who are Mexican American. Although the two sets of grandparents are different in many ways, they also have a great deal in common—in particular, their love for their granddaughter. The depth and joy of both cultures are conveyed in Spanish and English while we follow the narrator to the circus and the pier, share stories from her grandparents' pasts, and celebrate her birthday. This affirmation of both heritages will speak to all children who want to know more about their own families and ethnic backgrounds.

Blanco, A. (1998). *La estrella de Angel/Angel's kite.* San Francisco: Children's Book Press. (Ages: 4–8)

A young kite maker makes a beautiful kite depicting his entire town, which has never been the same since the church bell disappeared. Angel flies his kite, and after an exciting chase, brings the bell back to town. With lyrical language and whimsical collages, *Angel's Kite* is a fanciful tale of a young boy's determination to transform his dreams into reality. This story shows a sense of community, hope, and perseverance. The text is written in both English and Spanish.

Brown, M.W. (1942). *The runaway bunny/El conejito andarín.* New York: HarperCollins. (Ages: Infant to preschool)

The story begins with a young bunny who decides to run away. "If you run away," said his mother, "I will run after you. For you are my little bunny." No matter how many forms the little bunny takes, his steadfast, adoring, protective mother finds a way of retrieving him. The rhythmic story infuses young readers with a complete sense of security, reassurance, and peace.

Cisneros, S. (1997). *Pelitos/Hairs.* New York: Dragonfly Books. (Ages 4–8.)

This bilingual book celebrates diversity through the different types of hair of each family member. The poetic language creates an affectionate picture of the family home and familial love.

Dorros, A. (1995). *Abuela.* New York: Dutton Children's Books. (Ages: 4–8)

This story is narrated by a Hispanic American girl who imagines she's rising into the air over the park and flying over Manhattan with her loving, rosy-cheeked abuela (grandmother). The author integrates Spanish words and phrases with English text through Abuela's dialogue. Although some phrases are translated by the child, others will be understood in context. A glossary is also provided with definitions and pronunciations. This book is good for reading aloud to children or for newly independent readers to read alone. Although not bilingual in the strictest sense, this book is a less self-conscious, more artfully natural approach to multicultural material.

Gonzalez, L.M. (1999). *El gallo de bodas/The bossy gallito: A traditional Cuban folktale.* New York: Scholastic. (Ages: 4–8)

While walking to his uncle's wedding, a rooster cannot resist eating a piece of corn and thus dirties his beak. He must find a way to clean it before the wedding. This story highlights pridefulness and manners. This book contains a glossary of Spanish words and information about the different birds in the story.

Herrera, J.F. (2000). *The upside down boy/El niño de cabeza.* San Francisco: Children's Book Press. (Ages: 4–8)

The author tells the story of the year his migrant family settled down so that he could go to school for the first time. Juanito has a difficult time adjusting to his new school and misses the warmth of country life. Everything he does feels upside down: He eats lunch when it is recess, he goes out to play when it is time for lunch, and his tongue feels like a rock when he speaks English. Yet his sensitive teacher and loving family help him shine and find his place through poetry, art, and music. This text is printed in Spanish and English.

Jiménez, F. (1997). *The circuit: Stories from the life of a migrant child.* Albuquerque: University of New Mexico Press. (Ages: 12–17)

The Circuit is a collection of 12 independent but intertwined short stories that chronicle the experiences of a Mexican American family of migrant farm laborers as narrated by Panchito, one of the children. This is a powerful account of a family's journey to the fields of California and it describes how their lives are constantly moving, from strawberry fields to cotton fields, from tent cities to one-room shacks, from picking grapes to topping carrots and thinning lettuce. The story is told through the eyes of a boy who longs for an education and the right to call one place home. This is a story of survival, faith, and hope. It is a journey that will open readers' hearts and minds. This story is also published in Spanish.

Jiménez, F. (2000). *La mariposa.* Boston: Houghton Mifflin. (Ages: 4–8)

In his first year of school, Francisco can barely understand what his teacher says, but he is drawn to the silent, slow-moving caterpillar in the jar next to his desk. In order to find out how caterpillars turn into butterflies, Francisco studies the words in a butterfly book so many times that he can close his eyes and see the black letters, but he still cannot understand their meaning. This book gives an unsentimental account of Francisco's struggle to learn a language and reveals how powerful and sustaining our imaginations can be.

Joosse, B.M. (1998). *Mama, do you love me?/¿Me quieres, mamá?* San Francisco: Chronicle Books. (Ages: Infant to preschool)

This book tells a story about an Inuit daughter's attempt to find the limit of her mother's love. Her mother reassures her that her love is forever. There is a quiet joyfulness in the antics of the mother, daughter, and animals. Published in English and Spanish.

Lionni, L. (1973). *Frederick.* New York: Dragonfly Books. (Ages: 4–8)

While other mice are gathering food for the winter, Frederick seems to daydream the summer away. He concerns himself with art, and his friends grumble at his behavior. But when dreary winter comes, it is Frederick who warms his friends and cheers them with his words. Frederick's poetry is seen as essential for survival. Also available in Spanish.

Mora, P. (1998). *Pachanga deliciosa/Delicious hullabaloo.* Houston, TX: Piñata Books. (Ages: 4–8)

This is a story of a group of armadillos and lizards who host a party for their animal friends. It explores the meaning of friendship, working in collaboration, and celebrating around fun and food. The story is told in both English and Spanish.

Reiser, L. (1993). *Margaret and Margarita/Margarita y Margaret.* New York: Greenwillow Books. (Ages: 3–6)

Margaret, who speaks English, and Margarita, who speaks Spanish, meet on a trip to the park with their mothers. The language barrier immediately distances the adults, but soon the two little girls are chattering away. Each mother and daughter pair speaks the same or similar phrases in their own language on facing pages as the girls build a friendship.

Soto, G. (1996). *Too many tamales.* New York: Putnam Publishing Group. (Ages 4–8)

Maria is feeling so grown-up wearing her mother's apron and helping to knead the *masa* for the Christmas corn tamales. When her mother takes off her diamond ring so it will not become coated with the messy masa, Maria decides that life would be perfect if she could wear the ring, too. Trouble begins when she sneakily slips the sparkly ring on her thumb and resumes her kneading. Uh oh. It is not until later that night, after all the tamales have been cooked and after all her cousins and relatives have arrived, that Maria suddenly realizes what must have happened to the precious ring.

Stevens, J.R. (1995). *Carlos and the Squash Plant/Carlos y la planta de calabaza.* Flagstaff, AZ: Rising Moon Books. (Ages: 4–8)

This is a story about Carlos, a boy who does not heed his mother's advice to wash the back of his ears and ends up having a squash plant growing out of his head. (A collection of four books is available.)

Winter, J. (1996). *Josefina.* San Diego: Harcourt Trade Publishers. (Ages: 4–8)

Josefina Aguilar is a real-life Mexican folk artist who makes and sells painted clay figures in a small village. The author imagines Josefina's life and has her sculpting figurines in groups and numbers, and the action builds toward a grand finale, with Josefina displaying her day's work as a clever countdown brings the story full circle. Readers will reinforce their command of numbers and get a taste of Mexican culture, too.

Resources for Identifying Culturally and Linguistically Diverse Children's Books

Roberts, L.C., & Hill, H.T. (2003). *Children's books that break gender role stereotypes.* Retrieved August 28, 2009, from http://journal.naeyc.org/btj/200303/Books4Children.pdf

Weston, M. (Ed.). (2002). *Diversity in children's lives: Children's books and classroom helps.* Chapel Hill: University of North Carolina, FPG Child Development Institute.

Appendix

English/Spanish Glossary of Familiar Words

Greetings

Welcome!	*¡Bienvenido!*
Thank you	*Gracias*
Hello	*Hola*
Good morning	*Buenos días*
Good afternoon	*Buenas tardes*

Months of the year (note that month names are lowercase in Spanish)

January	*enero*
February	*febrero*
March	*marzo*
April	*abril*
May	*mayo*
June	*junio*
July	*julio*
August	*agosto*
September	*setiembre*
October	*octubre*
November	*noviembre*
December	*diciembre*

Classroom materials and environment

Classroom	*La sala de clase, el salón, el aula*
Library	*La biblioteca*
Books	*Los libros*

Bookshelf	El estante
Window	La ventana
Blackboard	La pizarra, el pizarrón
Wall	La pared
Bathroom	El baño
Light	La luz
Ceiling	El techo
Paper	El papel
Pencil	El lápiz
Floor	El piso

Colors

Green	Verde
Red	Rojo
Pink	Rosa
Blue	Azul
White	Blanco
Black	Negro
Purple	Púrpura, morado, violeta
Yellow	Amarillo
Orange	Naranja
Brown	Marrón, café, pardo

Numbers

One	Uno
Two	Dos
Three	Tres
Four	Cuatro
Five	Cinco
Six	Seis
Seven	Siete
Eight	Ocho
Nine	Nueve
Ten	Diez

Cultural and Linguistic Diversity in Early Childhood Self-Assessment Scale

Cultural and Linguistic Diversity in Early Childhood Self-Assessment Scale

PART I

Please circle the number that indicates the extent to which you agree with the following statements.

What You Believe	Strongly disagree	Disagree	Uncertain	Agree	Strongly agree
1. My own cultural beliefs affect the way in which I serve children and families that are from cultures different than my own.	1	2	3	4	5
2. It is not necessary for me to be aware of the cultural and linguistic backgrounds of the children and families I serve in order to provide them with good services.	1	2	3	4	5
3. Regardless of the racial and ethnic makeup of the children I work with, it is important for all children to be aware of multicultural diversity.	1	2	3	4	5
4. If families want to be successful in getting services, then they need to learn to communicate in a more straightforward, direct manner.	1	2	3	4	5
5. All families should teach their children to be independent as early as possible.	1	2	3	4	5
6. Latino families are less trusting of the early intervention system and prefer to keep their young children at home.	1	2	3	4	5
7. It is the early childhood professional's responsibility to support children in maintaining their home language.	1	2	3	4	5
8. A teacher should incorporate activities into the curriculum that teach children about diversity.	1	2	3	4	5
9. Teaching and intervention methods need to be adapted to meet the needs of children who are culturally and linguistically diverse.	1	2	3	4	5

(continued)

What You Believe	Strongly disagree	Disagree	Uncertain	Agree	Strongly agree
10. Allowing a child to use his or her home language in the classroom/ program will slow down his or her acquisition of English.	1	2	3	4	5
11. All children should receive the same intervention strategies regardless of cultural differences.	1	2	3	4	5

PART II

Please circle the number that indicates the extent to which you agree with the accuracy of the following information.

What You Know	Disagree	Uncertain	Agree
12. The term *Hispanic* was introduced by the U.S. federal government to identify people whose heritage can be traced to any Spanish-speaking country.	1	2	3
13. Mexicans make up the largest percentage of Hispanics/Latinos in United States.	1	2	3
14. More than half of Hispanics/ Latinos living in the United States are high school graduates.	1	2	3
15. Looking directly at someone when he or she speaks to you indicates the listener is paying attention.	1	2	3
16. Verbal communication is the most important aspect of communication.	1	2	3
17. Using a family member, such as an older child, to interpret is a good strategy when you do not have bilingual staff.	1	2	3
18. An interpreter is basically the same as a translator.	1	2	3
19. When problem solving with a family, the professional should try to avoid talking about feelings or emotional issues.	1	2	3

(continued)

The New Voices ~ Nuevas Voces Guide to Cultural and Linguistic Diversity in Early Childhood
by Dina C. Castro, Betsy Ayankoya, and Christina Kasprzak

What You Know	Disagree	Uncertain	Agree
20. Families that help their preschool child too much can prevent him or her from becoming independent and consequently hold back his or her development.	1	2	3
21. Families from different cultural groups educate their children to be either independent or interdependent.	1	2	3
22. *Educación* in Latino cultures is different than the concept of *education* in mainstream U.S. culture.	1	2	3
23. The concept of *respeto* refers to the notion that individuals are given respect given their position in society or in a family.	1	2	3
24. Children learn a second language so quickly and easily that it is easy for them to be in an English-only environment.	1	2	3
25. The younger the child, the more skilled in acquiring a second language.	1	2	3
26. As long as a child becomes proficient in English, losing his or her home language should not affect him or her in any negative way.	1	2	3
27. It is not possible to appropriately assess a young English language learner without involving his or her family.	1	2	3
28. Children may go through a silent period while learning a second language, but this is not necessarily an indicator of a disability.	1	2	3
29. Multicultural practices emphasize how other countries or cultures are different from mainstream U.S. culture.	1	2	3

(continued)

What You Know	Disagree	Uncertain	Agree
30. Classrooms/programs with children that are not culturally diverse do not need multicultural practices.	1	2	3
31. Toddlers and preschoolers are not too young to notice racial or ethnic differences.	1	2	3

PART III

Please circle the number that indicates how often you practice the following. If you do not work directly with families and/or children but provide solely administrative, supervisory, or consultative support to direct service providers, please skip this section and complete Section IV.

What You Do	Rarely/never	Occasionally	Frequently
32. I ask about the cultural background of the families I serve (e.g., how the family celebrates their child's birthday).	1	2	3
33. I participate in activities that teach me about about other cultures (e.g., reading books about other cultures, attending cultural festivals).	1	2	3
34. When using an interpreter, I make sure to look at the family member during the conversation rather than the interpreter.	1	2	3
35. When using an interpreter, I meet in advance and debrief afterward with the interpreter to ensure we are prepared.	1	2	3
36. I feel confident when communicating with children and families from cultures different than my own.	1	2	3
37. I provide written information to families in their home language.	1	2	3
38. I adapt my practices to make them compatible with a family's cultural perspectives.	1	2	3
39. I create opportunities for the children I serve to share their customs and beliefs with me and others.	1	2	3

(continued)

What You Do	Rarely/never	Occasionally	Frequently
40. I ask the families I work with to share their cultural experiences with me.	1	2	3
41. I ask families how they prefer to communicate with me (written or verbal, English or home language, with or without an interpreter).	1	2	3
42. I invite families from diverse backgrounds to volunteer in the classroom/program.	1	2	3
43. I make available books and materials in the home languages of the children I serve.	1	2	3
44. I help families find books and materials in their home language to read to their children at home.	1	2	3
45. I encourage families to speak and read to their children in their home language to help their child learn.	1	2	3
46. I involve families in the process of developing activities to use in the classroom/program.	1	2	3
47. I plan curriculum/therapy/services taking into account children's cultural and language backgrounds as well as natural environments and developmental needs.	1	2	3
48. I review my physical space (classroom, therapy room, office) to ensure it has decorations that include people from diverse races, cultures, abilities, and ages.	1	2	3
49. I review my intervention materials (books, dolls, toys) to ensure they represent diverse races, cultures, ages, and abilities.	1	2	3
50. I expose children I serve to music, art, and foods of many cultures.	1	2	3
51. I conduct activities that enable children to learn about disabilities.	1	2	3

(continued)

52. What do you hope to gain from participating in the New Voices ~ Nuevas Voces program that will improve your work with children and families?

_____

_____

_____

_____

_____

_____

_____

_____

_____

_____

_____

_____

_____

_____

_____

If you are not an administrator, supervisor or consultant, you *do not* need to complete the *next* section. Thank you for completing this questionnaire.

PART IV

Please circle the number that indicates how often you recommend the following practices. If you do not provide administrative, supervisory, or consultative support to direct service providers, you do not need to complete this section.

What You Recommend	Rarely/never	Occasionally	Frequently
53. I recommend teachers/providers ask about the cultural background of families they serve (e.g., how the family celebrates their child's birthday).	1	2	3
54. I recommend teachers/providers participate in activities that teach them about other cultures (e.g., reading books about other cultures, attending cultural festivals).	1	2	3
55. I recommend teachers/providers make sure to look at the family members during a conversation in which they are using an interpreter.	1	2	3

(continued)

What You Recommend	Rarely/never	Occasionally	Frequently
56. I recommend teachers/providers meet in advance and debrief afterward with an interpreter to ensure that everyone is prepared.	1	2	3
57. I recommend teachers/providers work on skills for communicating with children and families from cultures different than their own.	1	2	3
58. I recommend teachers/providers provide written information to families in their home language.	1	2	3
59. I recommend teachers/providers adapt their practices to make them compatible with a family's cultural perspectives.	1	2	3
60. I recommend teachers/providers create opportunities for children to share their customs and beliefs with them and others.	1	2	3
61. I recommend teachers/providers ask families to share their cultural experiences with them.	1	2	3
62. I recommend teachers/providers ask families how they prefer to communicate with them (written or verbal, English or home language, with or without an interpreter).	1	2	3
63. I recommend teachers/providers invite families from diverse backgrounds to volunteer in the classroom/program.	1	2	3
64. I recommend teachers/providers make available books and materials in the home languages of the children they serve.	1	2	3
65. I recommend teachers/providers help families find books and materials in their home language to read to their children at home.	1	2	3

(continued)

What You Recommend	Rarely/never	Occasionally	Frequently
66. I recommend teachers/providers encourage families to speak and read to their children in their home language to help their child learn.	1	2	3
67. I recommend teachers/providers involve families in the process of developing activities to use in the classroom/program.	1	2	3
68. I recommend teachers/providers plan curriculum/therapy/services taking into account children's cultural and language backgrounds as well as natural environments and developmental needs.	1	2	3
69. I recommend teachers/providers review their physical space (classroom, therapy room, office) to ensure it has decorations that include people from diverse races, cultures, abilities, and ages.	1	2	3
70. I recommend teachers/providers review their intervention materials (books, dolls, toys) to ensure they represent diverse races, cultures, ages, and abilities.	1	2	3
71. I recommend teachers/providers expose children they serve to music, art, and foods of many cultures.	1	2	3
72. I recommend teachers/providers conduct activities that enable children to learn about disabilities.	1	2	3

(continued)

73. What do you hope to gain from participating in the New Voices ~ Nuevas Voces program that will improve your work as an administrator, supervisor, or consultant?

_____

_____

_____

_____

_____

_____

_____

_____

_____

_____

_____

_____

_____

_____

Thank you for completing this questionnaire.

Response Key for the Cultural and Linguistic Diversity in Early Childhood Self-Assessment Scale

NEW VOICES

N V

NUEVAS VOCES

APPENDIX B

Response Key for the Cultural and Linguistic Diversity in Early Childhood Self-Assessment Scale

Directions: For each item where your answer matches the key response, give yourself 1 point.

PART I: What You Believe (Items 1–11):

Item number	Key response	Place 1 point in this column if your answer matches the key
1	4 or 5	
2	1 or 2	
3	4 or 5	
4	1 or 2	
5	1 or 2	
6	1 or 2	
7	4 or 5	
8	4 or 5	
9	4 or 5	
10	1 or 2	
11	1 or 2	

Total number of your Part I responses that match the Part I key responses: _____

PART II: What You Know (Items 12–31):

Item number	Key response	Place 1 point in this column if your answer matches the key
12	3	
13	3	
14	3	
15	1	
16	1	
17	1	
18	1	
19	1	
20	1	
21	1	
22	3	
23	3	
24	1	
25	1	
26	1	
27	3	

(continued)

Item number	Key response	Place 1 point in this column if your answer matches the key
28	3	
29	1	
30	1	
31	3	
Total number of your Part II responses that match the Part II key responses: _____		

PART III: **What You Do** (Items 32–52):

Item number	Key response	Place 1 point in this column if your answer matches the key
32	3	
33	3	
34	3	
35	3	
36	3	
37	3	
38	3	
39	3	
40	3	
41	3	
42	3	
43	3	
44	3	
45	3	
46	3	
47	3	
48	3	
49	3	
50	3	
51	3	
(*Note:* Item 52 is open ended, so there is no correct answer or point value assigned for this response.)		
Total number of your Part III responses that match the Part III key responses: _____		

(continued)

PART IV: What You Recommend (Items 53–73):

Item number	Key response	Place 1 point in this column if your answer matches the key
53	3	
54	3	
55	3	
56	3	
57	3	
58	3	
59	3	
60	3	
61	3	
62	3	
63	3	
64	3	
65	3	
66	3	
67	3	
68	3	
69	3	
70	3	
71	3	
72	3	

(*Note:* Item 73 is open ended, so there is no correct answer or point value assigned for this response.)

Total number of your Part IV responses that match the Part IV key responses: _____

(continued)

Total Score

Add the total number of correct responses from the corresponding key.

Part number	Number of correct responses
Part I	
Part II	
Part III (completed by direct service providers only)	
Part IV (completed by administrators, supervisors, or consultants only)	
Total number of correct responses (Note: If you have both roles—direct service provider and administrator, supervisor, or consultant—you completed Parts I–IV.)	

Number of correct responses

If you completed Parts I–III, the total number of possible matches to the key responses is 51.
If you completed Parts I, II and IV, the total number of possible matches to the key responses is 51.
If you completed Parts I–IV, the total number of possible matches to the key responses is 71.

Interpret Your Score

If you completed Parts I–III or Parts I, II, and IV:

Less than 19	Beginning
20–40	Intermediate
41–51	Advanced

If you completed Parts I–IV:

Less than 35	Beginning
36–50	Intermediate
51–71	Advanced

Next Steps

Review your self-assessment results and consider the following:
- Identify areas that are your strengths and areas where you might improve.
- Engage in the module work and focus on areas where you are not as strong.
- Obtain the recommended resources for more content and experiential activities that will focus on areas where you most want to increase your knowledge, attitudes, and skills.
- Develop an action plan related to each module to help you get started with implementing new skills and strategies in your everyday work (see Appendix D).
- Beginners might want to focus on foundational key attitudes and knowledge. As you increase your knowledge and skills, you might want to obtain additional items from the recommended resources.
- Consider peer-to-peer support, discussion groups with colleagues, mentoring, and other activities that will support your personal and program development.

APPENDIX
C

Antibias Observation Checklist

New VOICES
N V
Nuevas VOICES

APPENDIX C

Antibias Observation Checklist

Name _____ Program _____

Location _____ Observer _____ Date _____

Use the following scale:

1 = None/never (0 observations)
2 = Few/rarely (1–2 observations)

3 = Some/sometimes (3–4 observations)
4 = Many/often (more than 4 observations)

Visual/aesthetic environment (for office- and center-based settings only)

_____ 1.   There are images of children and adults from a variety of racial/ethnic groups, both from the community and U.S. society.

_____ 2.   There are images of people who have different abilities doing work and accompanying their families during recreational activities.

_____ 3.   There are images of children and/or families in the program (used with permission).

Materials and activities

____ 4.   Materials (e.g., books, toys, card games, puzzles, dolls) show diversity in

_____ 4a.   Racial backgrounds

_____ 4b.   Cultural backgrounds

_____ 4c.   Special needs and abilities

_____ 4d.   Languages

_____ 4e.   Gender roles

_____ 4f.   Family lifestyles

_____ 4g.   Occupations

_____ 4h.   Ages

_____ 5.   There are opportunities for children to see and hear various languages (e.g., labeling materials, alphabet and number posters, books, story tapes, songs, finger games).

_____ 6.   Materials reflect the language and culture of the child/family being served.

Interactions

_____ 7.   The teacher/provider interacts with the child in a way that is respectful of the family culture, including tone of voice, word choice, facial expressions, eye contact, and body language.

_____ 8.   The teacher/provider interacts with the family in a way that is respectful of the family culture, including tone of voice, word choice, facial expressions, eye contact, and body language.

_____ 9.   The teacher/provider interacts with the family in a way that takes into account the family's culture and individual needs.

_____ 10.   The teacher/provider uses (or attempts to use) the family's home language in greetings or other communication with child/family. (Skip this item if the observation session is not with a family whose language is diverse.)

(continued)

NV

_____ 11. The teacher/provider uses an interpreter effectively to communicate with family (e.g., the provider maintains eye contact with family, not the interpreter). (Skip this item if the observation session does not include an interpreter.)

_____ 12. The teacher/provider invites the parent/family to participate in decision making about the child's services (e.g., discuss the child's progress, plan certain services, participate in the actual provision of services).

_____ 13. The teacher/provider approaches/resolves disagreements between provider and family in a positive, respectful manner. (Skip this item if there are no disagreements observed during the session.)

Adapted from Peisner-Feinberg, E. (1993). *Anti-Bias Environment Checklist* (Unpublished rating scale). Chapel Hill: The University of North Carolina at Chapel Hill. Copyright © 1993 by Ellen Peisner-Feinberg. Used by permission of Ellen Peisner-Feinberg.

APPENDIX

D

Action Plan

Action Plan

Name _____ Date _____

Long-term goal _____

_____

What actions will I take?	When?	What resources or supports will I need?

Index

Tables, figures, and boxes are noted by *t*, *f*, and *b*, respectively.